CUTTHROAT, A JOUNRAL OF THE ARTS

CUTTHROAT,
A JOURNAL
OF THE ARTS

Cutthroat
P.O. Box 2414
Durango, Colorado 81302

ISBN: 9780979563461

CUTTHROAT

CUTTHROAT,
A JOURNAL
OF THE ARTS

2013 JOY HARJO POETRY PRIZE
and
RICK DEMARINIS SHORT STORY PRIZE
$1250 1st & $250 2nd plus publication

JUDGES
T.R. Hummer, Poetry
Pam Houston, Short Fiction

GUIDELINES: Go to www.cutthroatmag.com and submit poems and stories through our online submission manager or submit through the mails. A **SASE for announcement of winners is REQUIRED for all mailed entries.** Submit up to **3 poems** (100 line limit/one poem per page) or **one short story** (5000 word limit/double spaced) in **12 point font. NO AUTHOR NAME ALLOWED ON ANY MS.** Mail-ins must have a cover sheet with author name, address, phone & email, title(s) of submission, SASE for announcement of winners (all mss. recycled). There is a $17 nonrefundable entry fee per submission. Make checks to *Ravens Word Writers*. Deadline: **October 15, 2013. UNPUBLISHED WORK ONLY!** No work that has already won a prize is eligible. No former *CUTTHROAT* prize-winning author may enter the contest he/or she has previously won. Enter as often as you wish. Multiple submissions okay, but we must be informed immediately of acceptances elsewhere. Finalists considered for publication. Winners published in *CUTTHROAT* and announced on our website, in *POETS & WRITERS* and *AWP CHRONICLE.* No relatives of or staff members of CUTTHROAT nor close friends, relatives and no students of judges are eligible to enter our contests. See www.cutthroatmag.com for more information. **WE RECOMMEND YOU READ A COPY OF CUTTHROAT BEFORE ENTERING OUR CONTESTS.**

CUTTHROAT,
A JOURNAL
OF THE ARTS

EDITOR IN CHIEF:	PAMELA USCHUK
FICTION EDITOR:	ELIZABETH ALVARADO
POETRY EDITOR:	WILLIAM PITT ROOT
ONLINE FICTION EDITOR:	WILLIAM LUVAAS
ASSISTANT POETRY EDITOR:	HOWIE FAERSTEIN
ASSISTANT FICTION EDITORS:	KINDALL GRAY
	ALSION McCABE
ASSISTANT EDITORS:	LAJLA CLINE
	JULIE JACOBSON

CONTRIBUTING EDITORS: Sandra Alcosser, Charles Baxter, Frank Bergon, Red Bird, Janet Burroway, Robert Olen Butler, Ram Devineni, Elizabeth Dewberry, Rick DeMarinis, Joy Harjo, Richard Jackson, Marilyn Kallet, Richard Katrovas, Zelda Lockhart, Demetria Martinez, John McNally, Jane Mead, Penelope Niven, Dennis Sampson, Rebecca Seiferle, and Lyrae van Clief-Stefanon.

Send submissions, subscription payments and inquiries to;
CUTTHROAT, A JOURNAL OF THE ARTS
P.O. Box 2124, Durango, Colorado, 81302
phone: 970-903-7914
email: cutthroatmag@gmail.co
Make checks to Raven's Word Writers Center or Cutthroat, A Journal of the Arts.
Subscriptions are $25 per two issues or $15 for a single issue.
We are self-funded so all **Donations gratefully accepted.**

CUTTHROAT CONGRATULATES

Brittney Scott of Richmond, VA
1st Prize, 2012 Joy Harjo Poetry Prize
"The Winter Following My Father's Death"
selected by Linda Gregerson

Laura Moretz of Winston-Salem, NC
1st Prize, 2012 Rick DeMarinis Short Fiction Prize
"Philo Goes Home"
selected by Charles Baxter

Don Judson of Attleboro, MA
2nd place, 2012 Joy Harjo Poetry Prize
"My Dog and I Decide to Sit Out the Next Debt Ceiling Fight,"
and
Mike Nelson of Kalamazoo, MI
2012 Honorable Mention, "Swim At Your Own Risk"

Elizabeth Evans of Tucson, AZ
2nd place, 2012 Rick DeMarinis Short Story Prize,
"Making Conversation,"
and
Andrea Lewis of Vashon, WA
2012 Honorable Mention,
'Cryonic Freeze"

OUR DEEP APPRECIATION TO ALL WRITERS WHO SUBMITTED
TO THIS YEAR'S WRITING COMPETITIONS!

2010 JOY HARJO POETRY CONTEST FINALISTS

"The Architects Were Crows," River L. Allen of Green Bay, WI
"Quaker Witness," Charles Atkinson of Soquel, CA
"We Show Each Other Our Scars," Devreaux Baker of Mendocino, CA
"Shapely," Tony Barnstone of Whittier, CA
"Defaced," Mary Pacifico Curtis of Los Gatos, CA
"Terrible Beauty," Mary Fitzpatrick of Pasadena, CA
"Clanging," Didi Goldenhar of Jackson Heights, NY
"Barrow," Anna Maxymiw of Toronto, Ontario, Canada
"Out of This World," Peter Nash of Petrolia, CA
"If There's A Gun In A Chekhov Story, It's Going To Go Off," Mike Nelson of Kalamazoo, MI
"Sunday Dress" and "Lusty Shoes," Emma Rose of New York, NY
"Hope," Dixie Salazar of Fresno, CA
"I Carry My Prayers Inside My Fists," Ann-erika White Bird of St. Francis, SD

2010 RICK DEMARINIS SHORT FICTION CONTEST FINALISTS

"The Heavens Hold," Anneliese Schultz of Richmond, British Columbia, Canada
"The Lives That Came Before, The Lives That Never End," Tara Wright of Menlo Park, CA
"In Rock Springs Where the Angel Trumpets Sound," Tom Pamperin of Chippewa Falls, WI
"Obsolescence," Raul Palma of Chicago, IL
"Cruz," Genevieve Thurtlesa of San Mateo, CA
"Bruno," Diane Stevens of Laredo, TX
"A Different Sized Us," David Armstrong of Las Vegas, NV
"Muneca," Amina Gautier of Chicago, IL
"Complicity," Jeffrey Schneider of Ellensvill, NY
"Trout and Crayfish," Karl Lunden of Fountain Hills, AZ
"Zhee Zhou," Anara Guard of Sacramento, CA
"In San Francisco," Terrence Cheng of Bronx, NY
"Impact," Sandi Wallace of Victoria, Australia
"The Ox and The Ant," Nancy Williard of June Lake, CA
"Inside Voice," Aaron Tillman of West Roxbury, MA

CUTTHROAT contents

2012 JOY HARJO POETRY PRIZE

Brittney Scott

THE WINTER FOLLOWING MY FATHER'S DEATH

The deer came dressed as bone
because snow, winter's best linen,
silently buried the food.
He lies on the concrete in the wildlife rescue
pumping straw-stalk legs.
I've thrown myself over him,
my ribs on his, two brittle cages,
while the vet shaves a patch of fur.
She tries to keep his rolling veins steady.
He is young, maybe his first frost
foraging without a mother, without antlers,
hauling an endless hunger.

Blood wells where the needle pulls.
Will a deer bruise, will it grieve
those painful colors?
I have to hold his head up or he will choke
when we try to tube feed.
His neck is so long and graceful
I know I would paint it stiff, stunted.
His neck, a wobbling
ballerina. And his barely blinking
black eye is nowhere close
to here. It sees field,

the opening in the wood's break.
It is true that deer do not see red,
but their vision cuts through dark,
perceives a blue more brilliant than any
artist's mineral. This deer must know my face
as two cobalt burns, as moonlike.

My muscles fade into numbness,
it is just this deer I feel, our bodies
dredged from roadside
river ditches. The wildlife
always listening. And then
his nostrils puff no more invitations
and I don't even notice at first, his
death like I round a corner and
swerve into a stranger that says
he knows me
better than I know myself.

Don Judson

My Dog and I Decide to Sit Out the Next Debt Ceiling Fight

the older boys would sneer, Don't believe nothin' they meant
anything who knew how right they were running up and down
all these same streets each night a finger in someones sisters
pockets so certainly not me believing in my long dead father
sitting quietly there at a corner window kitchen table knitting
his fingers furiously stunned to have stumbled artless

back to all of us once more but belief is important to get from
A to B so I choose to believe in my dog chasing baseballs across
the grass one block from Dunkin Doughnuts and just behind our
very own low income housing project we're all pretty happy and
beautiful trees footing long deep shadows and those sharp cuts
of light flowing and certainly too the birds who veer as they have
and always will plus most of all our very own job creators giving
everything one final shove right there on tv and wearing us like a
grey shark-skin suit yet truly and always it is long past gone

father father without end alone who dreams this world
elbow crawling once again japanese horror movie style
out some goddamn haunted-house door

so my oh my! here comes daddy again throwing little old
childhood me down the cellar stairs his quick fists his presence
looming but (like all of us must) growing old and weak so that
daddy hunched over working a drain in the bathtub has told me
to give a hand is the one I stand over hammer cocked
waiting for him to look up waiting for him to make it real

Mike Nelson

SWIM AT YOUR OWN RISK

The birds are angry tonight
in the jailhouse of broken hearts, and the worm's
just a guest of the apple core.
The leaves don't know either. They
are silences. They are an ocean whispering
into the One. The cracks in the sidewalk are dark,
but you remember a shirt you wore twenty years ago,
the sleeves cut off, yellow letters enticing
EAT THE WORM /Monte Alban
Mezcal. You remember wallowing in
yourself all one timeless morning
in the drunk tank, the intractable clanging
of doors, your inner voice amongst the din
of other voices and metal. No sun came.
Even the bare bulbs had cages.
Inside the doorless toilet stall, one bird was helping another out
with the tobacco and papers he'd smuggled in
in a plastic baggie in his anus.
Muffled groans. Then it was another's brilliant idea
to cover a light bulb with his T-shirt
so he could gently break it
and, basically, hotwire a cigarette.
Someone else had a length of string.
So a smoke could be passed to the holding cell
next door. So money was exchanged. And pills.
And knowledge. You? It seemed you were alone
and far from the woods where you once played,
and ruminated, and found the neighbor girl's dog, Half Pint,
dead in the dry creek bed. But you
were not far. How tell her? A dry creek
makes no sound, unless it's the sound the leaves make,
fallen into it, as you walk on them. Rusty landlocked
hulks—boats? hearts? corpseless empty cells?—

all around. Some nights the boy you were woke all at once
to the sound of rain and wind and trees swaying
and the dark out there growing
larger all the time. Sometimes you woke
in the morning, gradually, the calls of birds
a creek flowing by—a sound the mind makes, what the mind
makes of sound.

2010 RICK DEMARINIS SHORT STORY PRIZE

Laura Moretz

PHILO GOES HOME

They gassed up at a Wilco station in North Wilkesboro. Philomel watched Martha pull back onto U.S. 421, balancing a Styrofoam coffee cup on top of the wheel as she made the two-handed maneuver. Martha took her license for granted. A judge would decide if Philo ever drove again. A year sober, Philo wanted to see her oldest sons, and this had propelled her to ask Martha, the only other 28-year-old woman she'd met in AA, to drive her home.

Martha said, "Tell me about Daniel." Martha didn't usually ask Philo for stories about the past. Now she wanted to know about the boys' father, the one who died.

"You want the pretty stuff or the ugly stuff?" Philo asked.

"Pretty first," Martha said. "Ugly, up to you."

"Daniel asked me out when he started to drive. He'd rebuilt a Datsun, and he swooped around curves like a crazy man. One time he and his friends set up a bathtub on a mountainside."

Martha laughed.

"No, really! They carried it almost a mile to a pine grove, set it on some rocks, and filled it with buckets of creek water. They built a fire under the tub to warm it, not for cooking, but for bathing, and by the time Daniel brought me there, the flames were out but the water was still warm, and we bathed under the stars in that white claw-foot tub in the springtime. We had a six-pack, and a couple of blankets. He asked me to marry him there. I was probably pregnant already, but I didn't know it."

"That's a pretty scene to imagine, a warm bath on a mountainside," Martha said.

Twelve years ago, Philo couldn't imagine being with anyone else, ever. She had counted the starry freckles on Daniel's plump shoulders as if they were a permanent map of the heavens.

Philo had already told Martha how Daniel died. His Datsun went off a cliff at the work site for the Linn Cove Viaduct, the last segment

6

of the Blue Ridge Parkway, the section that swings out over air to get around the cliffs. By day, he'd poured concrete there. One night he flew off it, over the trees, and crashed. The insurance company ruled his death accidental. Philo didn't tell them he was high on coke, he'd been talking crazy and laughing about flying and dying that very night, and that his friends couldn't get his car keys from him. If she'd been a casual drug user and drinker before his death, after his death she turned professional. The settlement money went for house parties and cocaine for two years until the money was gone, and she begged the Gammas to take the boys so she could join a paint crew in Greensboro. Gamma Nan told Philo then that if she ever tried to take the boys back, she'd report her has an unfit mother. Philo had yet to ask her if she'd changed her mind.

Martha's Tercel emerged from under the stone bridge that suspended the Blue Ridge Parkway and came to an intersection. "Do I turn left?" Martha asked.

"Yes." Martha didn't need to know all the ugly parts. What would Martha think if she knew about Daniel drunk and shoving her, about Philo drunk and high and ignoring her babies, the kind of things she hated to recall? Martha knew enough.

Martha said, "The past is like a dream isn't it? The pretty parts?"

"Uh huh," Philo said. She guided Martha through Boone, past a new shopping center that had sprung up like summer mushrooms and a gas station that had been there forever with the same Esso sign in back and the new Exxon sign in front. They drove past Watauga High School and on toward Avery County. Martha said she could breathe better less than a hundred miles from Greensboro.

Not Philo. She felt her ribs clamping in on her heart and lungs because she was headed to the place where the Gammas—her grandmother, mother, and aunt—acted like the three fates and collected checks for Aid to Dependent Children in addition to the little she sent. Dense forest rose up, gashed by new roads that led to mammoth vacation homes.

"How are you feeling?" Martha asked.

"Like I want to throw up," Philo said, and laughed a tight laugh.

Still, Philo pointed out landmarks as they went—Lees-McRae College in Banner Elk, Beech Mountain, and apartment complexes and restaurants she'd painted with her first paint crew, the one she'd followed down to Greensboro. The men had treated her like one of the guys, she thought then, but looking back, they'd protected her, too—not that she needed it. She worked harder than any of them. In Avery County, the mountains humped up like spiny-backed beasts; ice and frozen crusts of snow edged the thin highway. "Slow down," Philo said. "You turn up ahead. There."

Martha made a sharp right turn up a skinny iced road through a piney forest that opened into a boulder-strewn field. The sun hit the road there, and the ice had turned to loose slush. Martha had no trouble getting up the steepest part to Philo's family home.

"So it's Evan, 11, and Sam, 7, right?" Martha asked as she sprung her seat belt.

"Right," Philo said, exhaling. "We'll see how this goes."

The door was never locked. Philo led Martha into the curtained darkness of the living room. The air smelled like wet firewood. Three women sat in dark leather recliners, backs to the blindered windows, watching something with a laugh track, turned low. Gamma Mae was attached to her oxygen tank. Every breath sounded like wind through a tunnel. Gamma Nan sat erect between Mae and Jean. Nan was widow and matriarch ever since her husband's tractor turned over on him in a ditch when Mae and Jean were small. The women didn't stir, though surely they'd noticed how the light changed when the door opened. Philo heard a ping, ping, ping sound to the right, a music that meant the boys were playing a video game, so she shouted out "Hey" to the Gammas, and left Martha to fend for herself. She turned the loose glass knob of the front bedroom.

"Hey, boys," she said. Sam flew at her, but Evan didn't budge from his game.

"Mama, Mama," Sam said, like it hadn't been over a year.

Evan glanced over. "Hey," he said with half a shrug.

"Hey," Philo said, willing to wait it out. Sam danced around her, jumping high to clasp her. "Whoa there, buckaroo," she said. He climbed on the four-poster bed and swayed over her like a giant. "OK, OK," she said, laughing. "What's going on in your game, Evan?"

Sam answered for him. "Super Mario has to jump and get stars and watch out for bad guys and make it all the way through this world to get to a new level, Mama. Are you staying, Mama?"

"I'm staying tonight," Philo said, "but first we're going to get some lunch. Do you want pizza, Evan?"

Evan stared at his game. "Yeah," he said.

"Watch out Mario," Sam said. "Ha, ha, he's dead! Turn it off, Evan!"

Evan switched it off. "Hi, Mama," he said. Eleven was awkward for him. Easy enough for Philo to treat him like one of the guys she worked with, low key, no emotion, just do the job at hand.

"I brought a friend. She drove me," Philo said, leading the boys into the gloomy living room. Martha, teetering on a couch armrest near Gamma Jean and Gamma Nan, talked high and swervy like the flute of a snake charmer. Philo heard: *Ocean … mountains … home.* Gamma Mae's wheezy breath moved fast through the tube, like she was trying to access enough to talk. Gamma Nan tilted her head at Martha, maybe entranced, or maybe just stretching out the stiff neck she'd always complained about. Gamma Jean, Philo's mother, kept her eyes on the television. Her pain pills held her hostage most of the time. Philo couldn't remember the source of the pain that had led to the pills.

Philo stayed with the boys, near the front door. "Martha," she said, and Martha turned quickly. The Gammas didn't seem to hear Philo.

"Excuse me," Martha said to the Gamma Nan, with a crisp voice and a smile, and went to Philo.

Philo said, "Mama, Gamma Nan, we're going out with the boys."

The Gammas didn't speak, which Philo took as approval, or as close as she would get.

On the porch, Martha appraised the boys' outerwear like a school marm. "Zip up boys. Tie your shoes," and Sam did it, but Evan gave her a look like *where did you come from?* Then, slowly, he squatted down, tightened his laces, and tied his boots.

"Are we getting in that car?" Sam asked Philo, pointing at Martha's Tercel by the steps.

"Yes," Philo said, ruffling his hair. Like a dog eager for affection, he leaned into her hand.

"Who's driving?" Evan asked.

"It's Martha's car—she'll drive, honey." Evan winced at the *honey.* "You want pizza?"

"Pizza, pizza!" Sam jumped frenetically.

Martha released her bucket seat, and the boys got in. "I require seat belts," she said. Did the Gammas require that? Did the old women drive anymore? The boys complied. Evan leaned sideways to help Sam find the fastener which was crammed between the seat and seatback. Philo couldn't see her boys from the front seat, which made it harder to talk. Several topics wouldn't do—Joey, the new brother they hadn't met; Harrell, the new husband they hadn't met either; or her struggle to stay clean, which was really none of their business.

"I hope there's not too much dog hair back there," Martha said. "When I take my dog to a park, she gets in the back and run back and forth like she's getting ready for a race."

Sam laughed. "I want a dog but Gamma Nan says we can't feed no dog it's hard enough feeding us, she says."

"Shut up, Sam," Evan said.

Martha fiddled with the radio but got only static. Sam started bouncing again, like a jack-in-the-box with a lid that wouldn't fasten. Evan put a hand on his thigh, and Sam yelled, "Hey!"

Evan said, "Shush." Philo concentrated on the road.

The pizza place was in the downtown stretch of Newland by some railroad tracks, a thin, deep restaurant with tall-backed booths and old Coke signs nailed to the walls and the smell of baking crust in the air. Philo ordered a large pizza to share, milkshakes for the boys, and french fries. Martha asked for a Diet Coke.

"Do you remember coming here?" Philo asked Evan. He nodded slightly.

Sam said, "I don't remember." He stood up on the bench of the booth and bent his knees to jump.

"Sit down," Evan said. "He'll settle down when there's food," he added. Likely, Evan kept Sam out of the Gammas' sights daily. Philo hid from the same women when she was young. Gamma Mae was Gamma Nan's top lieutenant then, the task master who told Philo to mop the kitchen floor with bleach that made Philo gag, and who punished her the next day for using bleach. Philo left at 16 to marry Daniel.

"What do you like to do, Evan?" Philo squirmed at her own question, the kind of question preachers asked in counseling sessions, not the kind of question a mother should have to ask.

"I like hunting," he said. "We saw a bear up on the mountain last summer. I want to hunt that bear."

"Where was the bear?"

"In the blackberry clearing. I followed it, but it was fast."

"You have a gun?"

"The Gammas got guns. Don't let me shoot none—don't want to teach me." His eyes flitted to hers briefly.

"Probably don't know how to shoot either," Philo said.

"Probably not." They were in league against the Gammas.

The waitress came with two vanilla milkshakes, and Sam's eyes went wide with excitement. He ripped off part of the paper on his straw and blew the rest of the paper up in the air like confetti. It landed on

Martha's shoulder, and she brushed it off. Sam stuck the straw in the thick goop and started sucking.

"See?" Evan said. "Now he'll be quiet."

"What about school?" Philo asked.

"What about it?" Evan said. "It's boring. It's school." He arched his back and interlocked his fingers behind his head like a grown man.

Martha took polite sips of her Diet Coke, and then shook a little salt from a shaker onto the table. She looped her hair behind her ears, then tried to balance the edge of the shaker's base on a few grains, squinting with concentration. She did the same thing when she and Philo had coffee with others after their meetings. When she let go, it stayed there, balanced.

"Let me try," Sam said, and he tried. He whooped when the shaker fell over.

The waitress brought the pizza, with pepperoni and sausage, and the french fries. Martha nibbled on a slice after dabbing grease off the top with a paper napkin. Philo watched the boys tear into theirs.

"I miss you boys," Philo said.

"Yeah?" Evan said, a challenge.

"Mama, Mama!" Sam said.

"Shush," Evan said.

Toward the end of the pizza, the boys slowed down.

"I'm going to throw up," Sam said.

"Stop eating, Sam," Evan said, shoving the pizza and French fries away from him.

Philo dreaded going back to the house and the dim living room where the Gammas were probably watching reruns of "Little House on the Prairie." "Martha, do you mind a little side trip?" she asked when they got back in the car.

"Just tell me where to turn," Martha said.

Sam moaned and laid his head on the backseat.

"Sam needs to throw up," Evan said. Martha pulled over on a thin shoulder next to a narrow ditch. The mountainside went up fast beyond it. Philo jumped out, and Evan pulled out Sam, who threw up with his brother holding him. Martha stayed in the car. Philo found a pack of Kleenex in her purse and handed it to the boy. He wiped his mouth and handed the tissues back to her. She balled up the vomit-stained tissues and smushed them into her pocket.

"Mama, I want more pizza," he said.

"You're crazy, Sam." Philo hugged his bony collection of angles, and he collapsed against her.

Back in the car, Philo told Martha to take the next turn.

"Where are we going?" Evan asked.

"To the cemetery," Philo said.

The boys were quiet then, and Martha drove up another hill steeper than the road to their house but cleared of ice and snow by the state. At the top, the mountainside graveyard was treeless and tilted its face west toward the sun which had melted some of the snow.

"Are we looking for Daddy's gravestone?" Sam asked.

Philo nodded. "Didn't bring flowers or nothing. Just want to visit."

The boy's feet sunk in the wet snow as they set out with Philo, Martha holding back. "I don't have boots," she said. "I'm staying here."

"We won't be long," Philo said.

"Where is it, Mama?" Sam asked. He looked back at the tracks he'd left behind him. He tried herringbone steps and walking backwards.

"Down at the end. The Johnson plot was full. We started a new plot for him." Their feet crunched in syncopation. Philo hadn't been here since the burial, when she held the infant Sam during the blur of preacher talk, during all the hymns. Under the funeral home tent, midsummer sweat rolled down her face, but she couldn't cry. *She's in shock,* Gamma Mae said.

The deputies questioned her the night his car soared off the mountain. She knew them from when they'd shut down parties or sent her and Daniel home from parking-lot hangouts. Only natural to freeze them out. *Don't say nothing. They don't need to know nothing.* But her fake smiles and her shrugs had left her with questions, too. She'd never know if he'd meant to do it, if he'd done it if he wasn't high, if it was a true accident.

The melting snow seeped through Philo's thin canvas sneakers and her socks absorbed the ice water. Snow clung to the bottom of her jeans. She got to where the marker should be, but couldn't guess exactly where the flat stone lay. "Boys, help me find it."

"I thought gravestones stood up," Sam said.

"Stand-up stones cost more," Philo said.

"So his stone's lying down."

"That's right." Philo wedged a foot in the snow and ice and pushed some aside, but uncovered only dead grass.

"It's where the snow dips in like craters—that's where the stones are," Evan said. His boots cleared several quickly. His down vest hung open like cold didn't bother him. "Daniel Johnson. Here he is."

Sam ran over. "That's Daddy?" he said.

"It's a piece of stone, Sam," Evan said.

"He's under there?"

"Just ashes, baby," Philo said. There wasn't much of Daniel left after the car caught fire, but Philo asked for the bones, whatever they found, to cremate and bury.

"A kid at school told me my Dad was stupid for trying to fly off the mountain," Sam said, looking at the stone as if it knew the answer.

"Tell the kid it was an accident," Philo said.

"That's what I said, but he went on and on."

"Who?" Evan asked, looking out over the valley.

"Stu Carpenter."

"His brother said the same thing to me. I pounded him," Evan said, his voice choking.

Philo felt a strange warmness in her eyes. "I wish your Dad could see you now."

"You found another husband. You replaced him." Evan spoke calmly, looking at his boots in the granular snow.

"Nah," Philo said, her face wet with tears. "I can't replace him neither. We all lost being a family. And I did it, too. I left."

"Mama, are you going to stay here with us?" Sam asked.

"Shut up, Sam." Evan glared at his brother.

"I can't," Philo said. She placed her hand on Evan's arm. He let her hand remain.

"Take me with you, then," Sam tugged on Philo's other arm. "Please, please, please."

Evan broke away toward the car.

"Martha's waiting for us," Philo said. She lifted her sopping, heavy feet. The whole earth was melting its frozen shell, and she was absorbing its weight.

The grey hulk of house was in the shadow of the mountain when they drove back up the freezing slush driveway. Philo grabbed her change of clothes from the car, and Martha took her blue canvas bag. The boys ran up the steps ahead of them and into the front bedroom where Philo had found them that morning. Philo showed Martha where they could sleep in the attic bedroom at the front of the house. The boys slept in the back attic bedroom. Philo changed into dry pants and socks. Martha pulled a book out of her bag, *The Cider House Rules*. "I guess I should be social with your family downstairs," Martha said.

"Those old women? Well, they do seem to like you. But they don't expect nothing."

"I'll be down in a bit," Martha said, sitting on her bed.

Philo went downstairs to the boys.

"You're still wet!" she said. "Get on some dry clothes." Evan looked resentful, but he said, "Come on, Sam."

Philo went over to where the Gammas sat in their shiny leather recliners.

"You were gone a long time, Philomel," Gamma Nan said quietly.

"I took the boys up to the cemetery to visit Daniel's grave," she said.

"Under all that snow? How'd you find it?" Gamma Jean asked.

"We had to hunt, but Evan found it."

"Well," Gamma Mae drew wheezily on her oxygen and exhaled. "Well." Philo still flinched in Mae's presence, no matter that Mae would never chase her with a broom again.

"It's time you took a boy home," Gamma Nan said.

"One boy?" Philo asked.

"That's right. We'll tell you which tomorrow." Nan's pasty-white face didn't show emotion.

"I didn't think you'd trust me with either," Philo said.

"We're getting old, Philo, case you hadn't noticed."

"Seems like the boys should be together," Philo said. It wouldn't help to show how much she wanted them, but now that she'd seen how Evan looked out for Sam, it was hard to keep quiet. And there was this: She hadn't said word one to Harrell about bringing any boys home.

"It's one or none, Philomel. They can't both go at once. We'll tell you tomorrow."

Philo wanted to flip Gamma Nan out of her recliner. She wanted to yell about all the times she'd been beaten or hungry in this house, how she'd hid in the attic half her childhood, and how her boys probably suffered the same way, but instead she rose and went to Martha, who was in the kitchen. Philo remembered, too late, that food wasn't one of the things the Gammas stocked. Martha might expect a regular supper, which was too much to expect.

Martha looked in the refrigerator.

"I see biscuits," Martha said, pulling out a tube of Hungry Jack dough. "Could we make some biscuits?"

"If you're hungry, make some biscuits," Philo said.

"What about supper? Should I wait?"

"Go ahead and make some biscuits," Philo said. There wouldn't be a supper from an empty refrigerator. The Gammas ate what Meals On

Wheels brought them. Philo wished she'd thought of that and brought some food.

Philo found a cookie sheet for Martha to use and washed it and dried it for her.

"Well, the boys had a good lunch," Martha said, scrunching her face with confusion. She peeled the outer paper off the tube of biscuit dough. The fact that Martha couldn't comprehend a household with no plan for supper was exactly what Philo liked about Martha.

"Gamma Nan says I can take one of the boys home tomorrow, but they haven't decided which one," Philo said.

"Which one? They want to separate them?" Martha poked the exposed cardboard to split it at the seam, and the dough burst out.

"Just one now, then the other later," Philo felt queasy.

"You can't say which?"

"I left them, remember? They never said I could take them back."

"You're their mother, Philo."

"Not in their eyes. I'm a bad loss. Besides, they want to keep a boy around." Martha didn't need to know about the money.

Martha separated the biscuits and placed them on the sheet. She turned on the oven and put the sheet in it. Then she went back to the fridge. "Jelly and margarine is all there is."

"The boys like jelly biscuits," Philo said.

When the biscuits were ready, perfectly golden under Martha's watchful eye, Philo fed the boys in the kitchen, and Martha, wouldn't you know it, brought biscuits to the Gammas in their recliners and sat with them while they ate. She couldn't let the witches alone.

They went to bed far earlier than Philo usually did, soon after the boys went to bed, just to be out of the Gammas' realm downstairs. Just to make tomorrow and leaving come faster. Martha read for a while, then turned out the light. Without the noise of a television, Philo was stuck with her thoughts. Her limbs twisted from side to side, powered by a restless motor. If she took both boys back, the Gammas would lose all their income from Aid to Dependent Children. And Harrell—what would Harrell say about more kids to feed who weren't his own kids? When she was a kid, she'd hid in the dormer, the pocket of shadow between her bed and Martha's. A piece of her still hid in that shadow, afraid of the Gammas' wrath.

In the morning Philo went back Gamma Nan, her white hair flat, her face long and blank, a pink and grey crocheted blanket covering her legs. She smelled of talcum powder and vinegar. Philo sat on the arm of the couch where Martha had perched the day before. Gamma Nan cut her eyes sideways at Philo. "We don't want no more teenagers. Take Evan with you."

Philo said, "Seems like the boys need each other, maybe more than they need me."

"Will you take him or not?" Gamma Nan's voice pitched higher.

"Yes, I'll take him."

"Sam can go later."

Philo felt a sadness ball up in her chest. She wanted to run up the mountain and yell, she wanted to fight back, but that never worked with the Gammas. Instead she went upstairs to see if Evan was awake. The boys' door was closed, and she heard nothing inside. She sat on the top step near his door and waited an hour until Evan got up. He gasped in surprise to see her. She held a finger to her lips. Evan left the door cracked while he went to the bathroom, and she studied Sam's flung covers and curled legs in the half-shadowed room. Then she led Evan to the porch.

"Gamma Nan wants you to go with me, to live. If you want to, that is."

"What about Sam?"

"Sam can go later. Gamma Nan wants you to go first."

Evan, in boxers and a T-shirt, picked up a piece of firewood and threw it back on the stack. It clattered and rolled to the porch floor.

Philo lit a cigarette and pulled on it fast.

Evan stared off the porch and shivered. Philo wanted to wrap her arms around him, but instead she touched his arm. When he turned toward her, she saw tears in his eyes. Then he pushed past her, into the house and up the stairs. Philo waited outside. She stubbed out her cigarette. He came back fully dressed.

"Don't follow me," he said, running down the steps. He ran into the tree shadows. When he slipped on the ice that had refrozen over night, he spread his arms for balance, and Philo saw one of the Gammas' pistols in his right hand.

Don't follow me, but she had to follow. Philo got her coat and pushed on her damp sneakers. She hoped he was looking for bear, although bears seldom wandered out during a freeze. She went up the road and saw his tracks turn off toward the blackberry patch. When she got to the clearing ringed by blackberry stalks, Evan was there, the pistol loose in his hand. His curly hair stuck out every which way from sleep.

"I haven't been any kind of mother, Evan. I will do better if you come with me." She took a few steps toward him. His eyes were sad.

He didn't speak for a long moment. "Other boys at school, they go hunting with their fathers. They fish, and they camp. I thought if I could learn to hunt, I'd be like them."

Philo watched him. "I grew up with the Gammas, too. I hated having no Dad. For boys, it's worse."

He dangled the gun, his thumb looped in the trigger guard. "I don't even know how to load it."

"We'll just put it back," Philo said. He came to her, and they left the clearing together. If they came back in summer, the smell of ripe blackberries would draw them to pick. The thorny stalks would draw ribbons of blood on their skin when they reached inside the tangle. Maybe they would see the bear. She couldn't say about hunting.

Evan packed his clothing in two plastic grocery bags. He left the Nintendo so Sam could play Super Mario. When Sam got up, Evan poured him a bowl of Frosted Flakes. He mixed powdered milk with water in a jug to pour on top. Philo sat with Sam while he slurped the cereal, stopping a few times to grin at her, like she was a good dream that survived until morning.

"Sam, the Gammas said only one of you can go home with me at a time, and they're sending Evan first, to kind of pave the way." It sounded surprisingly reasonable.

Sam burst into tears. "I want to go, too," he said, jumping up.

Philo stood and held him. "I know Sam. I'll be back for you, soon as I can."

Sam broke away and ran upstairs. She hoped he would forgive her one more time.

Leaving quickly was the only way. Evan went to the Gammas. Philo hated he gave them any reverence, but knowing when to display respect, that was something, too. As they loaded their things, Sam stood on the porch, his nose pushed up against the screen. Evan waved once to his brother, then stared ahead like he was seeing the road out for the first time. Philo waved at Sam beyond the point he could see her.

A half mile before Boone, Evan said, "I thought they'd send the baby with you."

"Maybe he's not such a baby," Philo said. "He'll be all right."

"I didn't think you wanted me," he said.

"Guess you were wrong," she said. She turned and caught his quick half smile.

At a stoplight on the outskirts of Boone, a half dozen places to eat lined the highway toward Blowing Rock. She imagined Evan eating a stack of pancakes at Shoney's.

"Are you hungry, Evan?"

"Didn't eat yet," he said.

Philo followed her son through Shoney's double doors. He was almost as tall as she was, and his blond baby curls had turned thick, wiry and dark. She had no idea what came next, so she fixed her mind on one thing. When they got to Greensboro, she'd go to Goodwill and buy him a bed.

Linda Hogan

THE EYES OF THE ANIMALS

Looking into the eyes of the elephant
I am looking also into the eyes of the great land tortoise
with its life more than a hundred years
and I see the sand, the salt water from those eyes, the mouth,
claws, flippers, hoof, trunk, all on the way to any water,
across a changed world
where nothing is familiar.

And looking into the eyes of the mountain gorilla infant
holding green bamboo with her black hands
and fingernails so perfect,
the eyes look back at me
so unwillingly gentle and alive,
so unable to say, take me out of the fur
as the turtle cannot say, take from me the great shell
or the elephant its tusk or hoof.
It would say I am light, kind.
I am the same as you.

I see the red eyes of the tree frog,
climbing with yellow webbed feet
hanging on, calling out for rain.

Dear life, let's you and I talk
about the orangutan surrounded by shining fur
all amber jewel, golden eyes
copper arms stretched thin,
open and reaching, holding the emerald plant
and the shining light of morning.
A diamond cutter could not make anything so great
so needed
so needy
so desired and desirable
as this red ruby of a child. So,
dear life, protect this world.

Life, look into the eye of the whale. There are no words
a man can speak so great as theirs.

And then there are the eyes of the wolf.
A god was named for them
And when you see any of these you know
all they want is to live
    to survive, to care for their playful young
just as we do
knowing god is not who or what
or anything but all this, Life,
even the circle of fern is unfolding,
and the eyes of the universe
look back at you
with the true knowledge of what you are,
saying, *human, woman, man, child, savior*
this world, even your self
you must learn to love.

Linda Hogan

MERCY, THE WORD

How I miss the animals of the ocean,
in the depths that can't be measured
of my heart,
deeper than water, or a universe of dark matter.
I want mercy in this world

and I miss the trees
that are daily falling, the birds
here too early to survive,
but not the lies of our time.

There is something wrong with me
because seeing the suffering
makes me weep and then I write these words.
What I really wish to write is a love poem
to ocean, tree, bird, a lover,
not to condemn soldiers
who follow orders
sworn to a nation
instead of the demands of compassion.

You know, I tell people,
earth has the grace
to create caves of shining crystal
and shifting dunes, mountains
with waters falling from them.
Water has the blessing of skin
left always unbroken, never scarred.

> I need mercy
> to make life that easy in this world.
> If not that, I need to harden my edges
> but mercy is a word
> that leaves me open instead.

Sebastian Matthews
POST WRECK

The tremor of the crash
shimmering into the body—
from cracked-open feet
into split ribcage—
rattling awhile
then expiring.
Each day

out, you must
must not forget,
an excursion: keep
crossing ever-widening
circles of aftershock;
at each tripping
wave, awake.

Daniel Nathan Terry

UNLIKE, DOGS

after we've been weaned, we attempt to love the world
in stages, and so we touch, and so

we kiss, yes. And, yes, eventually we open
our mouths to other tongues and we take

each other's roses with all their perfume,
thorns and decay and transparent spit and dew

inside, beyond the white fence of our teeth
and tender garden of our palette, deep into the word—

the womb of the throat. But this, only after
we have reached out with tentative fingers

for a sleeve, a cuff, the rough skin on the back
of a hand we hope is stronger than ours. This only

after we have held it, at least for a moment—
but often hours, days—at arm's length.

Humans are so fearful of taking the world
into their mouths—the nights of black moths and blacker

moons, the swollen bud and urgent blood of the surging
oak, the light and all it obscures from our limited sight.

Danger. Everywhere. But nothing so frightening
as our need for some other from outside of our skin

to make it less painful to live within it. We need so much,
but come to it so slowly, examine and consider, weigh

in our hands and judge if even an inch of flesh
is worthy of the terrible act of opening

our bodies, of exposing our warm, dark
chambers within where we still hide like nightmared

children. But what can timid fingertips know
of the virtues or poisons contained in the mouth

of another? And so the dog, not of the first order, handless,
thumbless, with no way to hold on to anything—and so no need

to evolve—takes the world into his mouth. And comes
to know it—between his teeth,

comes to love or hate it upon his wide tongue.
And it is up to him whether he drops it into the dirt

and moves on, or gnaws it a while, strips it
of its skins and barriers, crushes it

lovingly in his thick-boned jaw, then opens wide
his maw, lets the wider world become another holy cell

of his own beloved body.

Daniel Nathan Terry

LUCKY

At dawn, in the middle of the street, I found a dead pup,
no more than three months old, still warm, head crushed
by a tire, mouth shattered, seeping a red silence

into the filthy blacktop. I turned my back on him,
cursed his blonde hide, crossed paws, ruined black lips
and mangled smile that couldn't grant five minutes

for me to wipe the sleep from my eyes, pour coffee,
notice him sitting up in the street, rush to rescue him
from the oncoming truck.

When I returned to bury him, I saw another face—a brother—
darker, thicker furred than his dead sibling,
curled against the cold body,

wasting his warmth on his beloved dead, but fearless
and waiting for me—to stretch from my sorrow
and lift him back into the arms of the living.

Daniel Nathan Terry

WHAT IT MEANS TO HER

Black paws and muzzle to the winter grass, she doesn't look up
the way I do to see if there is anything worth remembering
about our walk. But then, for her, all walks are one—

scents of yesterday's walk, and the day's before,
and day's before fill her nostrils as if all our days
are contained in this moment. So, as my eyes search

for things to remember—noticing what can
and can no longer be seen—she breathes in the child who cycled by
an hour ago, the robins that dug in the grass this morning,

the cold rain that fell last Tuesday—but without the troubling
human losses like *an hour ago, this morning,* and *last Tuesday.*
She misses nothing and nothing ever ends.

Daniel Nathan Terry

WALKING LUCKY THROUGH YELLOW FLOWERS

I read somewhere that dogs see the world in shades of gray,
with two exceptions: yellow and blue. What must it be like

to walk down this road, leashed to the man who loves you,
cars and windblown trash ghosting past you like a train

in a black and white movie, the sky above you an endless
road of azure, the gray grass beneath your paws littered

with stars?

2012 RICK DEMARINIS SHORT STORY PRIZE
SECOND PLACE

Elizabeth Evans
MAKING CONVERSATION

While she divides Charlotte's wet hair into sections with giant, plastic clips, the beautiful stylist explains what she feeds her dogs, vegans like herself: potatoes, carrots, ground flax seeds, pinto beans...

Her words rattle around in Charlotte's head, rattle around in the frankly dusty salon, a funky conversion of a small adobe bungalow from the 1920's or so, quiet today, the only person present besides Charlotte and the stylist a sumo-wrestler sized woman (another stylist) who sits tweezing her miniscule, black eyebrows at the station across the way.

That the styling room is the bungalow's former kitchen is indicated by those rusty spots on the linoleum that show where appliances once stood.

"And, then, brewer's yeast for B vitamins," the stylist says.

The stylist is known for spotlighting her fine-boned loveliness with eccentric touches. Today, she has painted orange clown-circles on her cheeks and run a broad white skunk's stripe across the top of her spiky black hair. Over a purple unitard, she wears a swamp-green tutu that sparkles with burgundy and baby blue sequins. The tutu rustles crisply against the back of the black vinyl chair in which Charlotte sits. *Crunch, crunch*, the stylist's yellow firefighter boots go as she steps on sequins come unglued from her tutu and leading like bread crumbs from the salon's front door and across the old hardwood floors and up to her station.

"I alter the mix, now and then, because certain ingredients shouldn't be served together. Beets are great, but too high-glycemic to add to a dish that already includes carrots."

You could not say that the stylist is imposing this dog food business on Charlotte. Charlotte asked. Fifteen years ago, when the regional medical center hired her as a grant writer, she read a book on making conversation, Let's Talk! and rule number one in Let's Talk! was, *Never ask questions that can be answered yes or no, or with one word,* and, really, what the stylist is saying was interesting enough to Charlotte—she and her husband and daughter do have a dog—but now Charlotte needs for the stylist to stop now. She needs for the stylist to ask, "How are you doing?" so that Charlotte can say, "Well, actually, my dad died."

The stylist's asking how Charlotte is doing is unlikely. Charlotte has come to the stylist probably fifteen times over the last two years and, as a rule, the woman asks her only two questions. Number One is a breathy, almost exasperated, "So, what is it we're doing today?" Number Two, after picking up a strand of Charlotte's hair, frowning at it, letting it fall: "So, what products are you're using at home?" Despite the stylist's strange lack of sociability, Charlotte still wants to tell her, "My father died." In fact, she feels an odd urge to tell absolutely everyone, as if their not knowing that her father is dead turns whatever they say to her into something said to another person, and not to this person whose father is dead. *My father died last week. I just got back to Tucson yesterday.* She longs to say this not only to her friends and colleagues—some of the latter whom she doesn't know well, despite having worked with them for years—but also to nice Ruben with the red bandana who is janitor in her building at University Medical Center, and Uri who sells her fresh fish at Rincon Market. Generally, she has managed to restrain herself. Still, back in Iowa, running errands for the reception after the funeral, and she stopped to fill her mother's car with gasoline, when a poor toothless guy at the register asked how she was doing, she did blurt, "Actually, I'm in town because my dad died."

In addition to wanting to let people know about the death, she wants for the people she tells to make a certain, limited type of response. *I'm sorry to hear that. What a shame.* She doesn't want much. *Thanks,* she'll say. She won't start in on the joy of greeting people at the funeral whose faces she had not seen since she was so small that she had to look *up* to see them or the insanity of her crack addicted sister prancing into the old family room, making a face of disgust and rattling the blue plastic box in her hand while, in a hopelessly supercilious voice, she announced to Charlotte, her brother, their newly widowed mother, and Charlotte's little girl, "The bag from the hospital had Dad's dentures in it! Re-*volting!* I trust no one will object if I pitch them?"

Too much sunlight comes in the big, old double-hung window beside the stylist's station. The window has no shade, only festoons of long ribbons of pleated foil, and crystals and sea shells and pierced pop caps and tiny stuffed dogs hanging on threads. The stylist must not notice the sun because she moves around, does not have to stay in one place, feel the heat accumulate. She says a sing-song, "Hold still, *please!*" and sets her hands firmly on Charlotte's shoulders, *presses.* Maybe she detected the sloshing in Charlotte's skull; Charlotte's skull as a front-loader washing machine in that first cycle when the clothes flop back and forth while the machine first wets them down.

Five days ago, when the telephone rang at two a.m., Charlotte assumed that it was her big sister, Diana, the drug addict. Both women lived in Tucson, Arizona, and such calls had been coming in regularly for over ten years—"I'm out in my garage, looking at the rafters, trying to decide which one would be best for hanging myself" or "Someday you may be glad I invested in a semi-automatic weapon!"—the sort of thing that Charlotte now knew to respond to not by driving across town, but by offering to call 911 or reading off the number for the suicide prevention hotline.

The call five days ago came not from Diana, but from their mother's Iowa neighbor. Once Charlotte understood that was the case, she knew that big rigs bore down on her. "Your mom wants to tell you something, Charlotte," the neighbor lady said. "Here she is, now. Mary, here's Charlotte."

Just the thought of that call makes Charlotte tighten her hands on the padded vinyl arms of the salon chair. She still can't conceive of what it was like for her mother, whose life as a wife had grown up around her individual self like a strangler fig, to have made such a call and gone on to say, her voice firm after an initial clearing, "He's gone, Charlotte." Charlotte still can't quite believe that she received such a call, stood in the moonlit dark, holding the receiver of the telephone that sat on the maple dresser from the boyhood bedroom of the husband who watched her so sadly from his side of the bed; or the fact that, grasping what her mother meant, she managed to make her own first words be the right words—thank god—"Oh, honey, I'm so sorry." *Honey.* She did not know that she ever before had called her mother *honey.* They had called her *honey,* her mother and father had.

What her mother went on to say was vague. "The doctors let me see him after they got him cleaned-up. He told me he was just awful tired, awful tired, and I should go home and get some sleep. Then they called me at the house an hour later. Was it an hour later?" she asked. In the background, the neighbor said, "About an hour, yes."

Cleaned-up. Charlotte didn't like to think what that meant.

"Please, honey," her mother said, then, "will you share the news with Diana? Richard's on his way here."

Her big brother. Before Charlotte could collect herself to telephone Diana with the news, Richard called. Richard still lived in Iowa, had gone into the family roofing business, even become a Republican. "She killed him!" Richard said. Diana did not need to ask who *she* was. Diana. "I'll never forgive her! Until the day I die!" Charlotte did not agree. A few minutes later, she telephoned the familiar number.

Diana was cranked up. There was crazy loud music in the background and she shouted and laughed hilariously, "HOLD ON, I CAN'T HEAR YOU!" and dropped the telephone, "WHO IS THIS? TALK LOUDER! HOLD ON A SEC, I CAN'T FIGURE OUT HOW TO TURN DOWN THIS FUCKING MUSIC! NOW, WHO IS THIS?" on and on, so that, in the end, Charlotte finally had to shout—preposterous—"IT'S CHARLOTTE! DAD IS *DEAD*, DIANA!"

Last night, her first night home since the funeral, after putting her ten year old daughter in bed, Charlotte told her husband, a kind but often distracted man, about her urge to tell people the news. "It's weird," she said.

"I doubt it's all that weird, sweetie."

They were in the kitchen. She sat leaned forward, her chin on the table top, which made her neck ache. She stayed that way, the discomfort feeling appropriate. "Maybe not," she said, her voice narrowed because of her posture, "but there's something narcissistic in it. For me, I mean." Because it seemed to her that she dumbly hoped to nibble the edges of condolences offered for her actual grief at her father's death and privately transform the edges into a balm to heal the lacerations left by the man's regular small and large cruelties toward herself and her sister.

"You're in shock," her husband said, and he went to the hall closet and brought back his heavy leather jacket, which he wrapped around her slumped back. "Sit up now." He drew the jacket's long arms around her and tied them in a loose knot, as if the jacket were a shawl.

It is true that the death was a shock. Everyone who knew her hardy father thought that he would live to be old-old; given medical advances, Charlotte had expected him to live to be at least ninety-three, the age at which his own father died. Instead, he was seventy-two.

"It sounds complicated at first, but I've got it down to an art," the stylist says. She bobs her head along with a song—an eerie repetitive thing, half cowboy tune, half techno—that the enormous, tattooed young woman sings while she goes on plucking her eyebrows, those pale bones beneath the skinny lines as big as cups. "I use a pressure cooker for the pinto beans and I keep them in quart freezer boxes with red tops. You have to have a freezer if you're going to commit to something like this. The rice I boil with the open kettle-method, and then drain it and rinse it to get rid of the starch so things don't get gummy, and that I put in plastic bags I flatten and stack in the freezer."

She has big, white teeth, a beautiful smile. You can buy teeth like that, now. It must make a difference, Charlotte thinks, being so lovely.

From past visits, Charlotte knows the names of the vegan dogs whose photos frame the station's mirror: Hector, Louise and Spiff. She also knows the names or identities of a number of human subjects in the mirror's photos. A mountain-man leaning on a red Cadillac is the stylist's boyfriend, Mikey. Here are various shots of Mikey and the stylist's parents plus the three dogs vacationing at Rocky Point last Easter. The parents on twin Harleys (the stylist is not so much younger than Charlotte, but Charlotte's father already was forty when she was born, set in his ways; the idea of him and her mother wanting to ride motorcycles or vacation with Charlotte and her family is enviable, but impossible). Charlotte could say that. When she agreed, Charlotte could say, *Yeah, we lost my dad last week.* Not *lost.* That always sounds weird, as if you might have misplaced someone. Lots of photos of lots of people at lots of picnics and barbecues where party tents offered deep shade away from bright swags of Arizona sun. A studio portrait of the face of a lovely greyhound in a Santa hat. Last fall, the stylist's mother—Cindy—stole the greyhound from the backyard of people who always left the dog outside, broiling weather or cold, without even water in a bowl. "A story with a happy ending!" Charlotte said when the stylist told her the story, but it did not seem to make the stylist like her more.

The stylist tilts her gorgeous face one way then the other. Looking at her own or Charlotte's reflection in the mirror? No matter how many pictures Charlotte tears from magazines in order to show the hip stylist the haircuts that she would like to try—no matter how many times she mentions the haircuts of other of the stylist's clients—by the time that the stylist whips the cape away from Charlotte's neck, she has given Charlotte a smoothly under-turned 'do that looks like something that belongs on the head of a woman on her way to a country club luncheon—someone like Charlotte's mother—so wrong that, outside the salon's front door, Charlotte must bend over at the waist and run her fingers through her hair, mess things up for a while.

32

Could it be, Charlotte has sometimes wondered, that the stylist means to reprimand her? Indicate that Charlotte doesn't know her proper place in the world? Look at her shoes, sticking out like potatoes beneath the salon's black cape. She should have changed her shoes. After lunch today, back at the house, she ran out to water a new citrus, and the shoes are speckled and smeared with mud. Next time, what Charlotte should do: Not ask the stylist anything about anything. That might make her feel better. But, really, the main thing that she should do is not come back at all. *Don't come back again,* she tells herself. *When it's time to pay and the girl at the reception desk asks, "When would you like to come in again?" just say, "I don't have my calendar with me so I'll have to wait on that," or even, "I won't be coming back."*

She does not like to see herself in the mirror at this salon. Too much light. Worse, today, she sees the beginnings of some of the same wrinkles that she saw around Diana's eyes, that deep one in her upper lip. Suppose that in some way she is like Diana? Affects people in the way that Diana does. She wonders about that sometimes. She thinks of how people stared at Diana at the Minneapolis airport when she and Hannah met up with Diana at the gate for the regional airline that would fly them to their old hometown. In a gesture that was, at heart, sweetly nostalgic, Diana wore on her scrawny shoulders the twin glass-eyed foxes, tiny droopy legs and claws dangling, that had belonged to their paternal grandmother. The backs of her hands were hatch-marked (from checking for bugs with an Exacto knife, Charlotte knew). Diana's voice climbed madly up and down its private scales in split seconds, shrieks turning heads, mutters making her transactions with the woman at the gate impossible. Charlotte had not slept since the call from her mother and, lacking a winter coat, had settled for adding an old down vest of her husband's to her rain coat. She knew she looked related to that wild woman who suddenly turned away from the ticketing agent and said to Charlotte's eight year old daugher, "And so we'll all feel a whole lot better real soon"—and began ticking though the names and properties of the pills she was rattling out of an unlabeled bottle and into a cupped palm, "here's your Hydrocodone, your Valium, your Xanax, that's the little coral one"—

Hannah knew about her aunt's problems, had seen them enacted in her living room, and so she only looked away from the pills, and out through the floor to ceiling windows at the men on the tarmac, moving cones, loading up luggage. "No need to get all pissy on me, Hannah!" Diana said. She winked at Charlotte as if they were a team against

Hannah before she tottered off down the gate to find a bar. Missed the plane. But then it was all right once they got to her mother's house. Everyone who came by her mother's house and showed up for the funeral knew that their father was dead. Charlotte hadn't needed to tell anyone. Such a relief. Everyone knew. Everyone was sorry.

The stylist stops cutting Charlotte's hair and steps away from the chair and begins to rap on the lower half of the big double-hung window. "Hey!" she says. "Hey!" She tries to unlock the window, but the lock is so old, so covered with paint. She raps on the glass again. "Evie," she says to the big stylist, "look at this dude out back. He's clipping his toe nails and throwing the damn things in the planter!"

Facing away from the window and out into the parking lot that serves the various businesses along the street, a man of indeterminate age is crouched forward on a long, concrete planter. Tan wind breaker. Wide and deep comb marks in his dark hair. "How gross is that, Evie?" the stylist says.

The big stylist sets her tweezers on the counter at the station before her and rises heavily from the client chair. Her breath is noisy, big puffs out of her nose, as she waddles over to the window. Charlotte hopes that she is one of those enormous people who revels in food, adores her many tattoos and piercings and the yards of black jersey that she wears and doesn't mind at all the sacks of pale flesh that fall out between her complicated drapery as she bends to the window.

The man sitting on the planter begins to work one of his feet back into a loafer. The big stylist says in a low, sexy voice, "He can come over to my place and throw his nail trimmings into *my* germamiums, anytime."

The beautiful stylist laughs and smiles fondly at her friend. "The word's geraniums, dummy, and you can't even see his face! Go tell him to stop it, Evie! Tell him the owner is going to lose it if he doesn't stop!"

The other woman laughs. Charlotte catches her eye in the mirror and smiles and says, "How you doing?" and she nods and returns to her station and resumes plucking her eyebrows. All that sunlight coming in through the big window makes Charlotte feel queasy. She can't remember who taught her not to ask the mourning person of the deceased, "How old was he or she?" since it might suggest that, if the deceased was old, there wasn't a need to feel so bad. On several occasions, she has read that to be of real help after a death, you should offer to do specific things for the bereaved; ask, "What day do you do your laundry?" and when the mourning person answers, say, "I'll be over to do the laundry that day," although that always has struck her as presumptuous. What she herself always says is, "Tell me exactly what I can do to help. Cooking, shopping, whatever."

Her mother did not come to the airport with Richard to fetch her and Diana and Hannah. "But she's doing fabulously," Richard said. "Wait 'til you see her." It was true that she did look wonderful when she greeted them in her big front hall. She wore a handsome, dark blue sheath and dark, low heels and simple gold studs. She dispensed hugs, but with an air of distant politeness. She might have been the private secretary to a high-ranking executive just now away on an important business trip.

"Isn't she fabulous?" Richard whispered to Charlotte. "She's been like this ever since!"

Charlotte fears that her mother's calm will not last. Her mother always has folded-up like a fan during discussions of deeply held convictions. "A person's beliefs are private," she will say when asked for whom she means to vote in an upcoming election, and Charlotte has long viewed this as a cover for her having no beliefs or being afraid to let hers be known, like a person who lives in a dictatorship.

Well: So maybe she would do well as a widow.

Things had gone off nicely enough, thanks largely to Richard. Diana did disappear into her old bedroom the moment that they arrived at the house, and she screamed outrageous obscenities if anyone made a peep near her door, but she was fine at the funeral the next day, and, basically, people were relieved that she retired to the garage during the gathering afterwards. When she finally did come inside—most of the guests gone—the rear of her skirt was covered with a large circle of gritty oil from sitting on the lawnmower. Hands like ice, she dragged Charlotte down the hall to their parents' big master bathroom. "You have to come, you have to come!" she said. "I have to tell you!" In the bathroom, several pairs of their father's socks—black, shrunken, forlorn—hung on one of the many towel racks, and Charlotte looked away from the yards of reflections caught in the mirrored walls and set to bundling the socks the way that her father had taught her to the time that he saw her do it all wrong. She never did the job without hearing him say, *Just the toes! Christ! Don't pull the cuffs up high or you ruin the elastic!* "You know what I figured out, Charlotte?" Diana cried in a joyful, jaggedy voice. She blew her nose into one of the fancy guest towels, blue bells embroidered on the front, that their mother earlier had fanned across the granite counter. She laughed and threw the towel into the sink. Charlotte couldn't bear to be in the room with her then. So many years of this sort of thing, late night calls and promises and Charlotte's helping her get into treatment and Diana's leaving treatment the next day, screaming into the telephone, *you're the one who is fucked up, Miss Priss, you think you know it all,* and now their father was dead, these were his black socks with little bits of fuzz on the toes, he wouldn't have wanted them out, and Charlotte found an empty drawer in that room's dozens of drawers that also held things like complimentary hotel shampoos and bras that their mother hadn't worn for years and a bunch of shoe horns (pink and tortoiseshell and black plastic and rusted metal) clipped together on a shower curtain ring.

Diana wrapped herself around Charlotte, crying, "But this is so cool, Charlotte! You have to listen!" She was choking on laughter and tears and snuffling and couldn't squeeze out whatever it was that she wanted to say. Terrible to be so repulsed when what mattered was that their dad was dead—still, Charlotte had to escape her sister's arms, she couldn't stop herself—though, as a cover, to make herself look helpful, she stepped to the toilet paper roller and gathered a bundle of tissue and handed it to Diana.

Diana made a face and noisily snorted back the mucous in her nose and swallowed it. "Yum, yum!" she said and smiled wickedly. "But will you just listen, Char?" Her face crunched up into a combination of laughing and crying. "Because I figured it out! Out in the garage, finishing off a very nice bottle of scotch that our father would have been too cheap to buy himself, I figured it out! What nobody else seems to get! The fucker *died* so the rest of us could grow up, bless his heart!"

Charlotte stuffed the toilet paper in her hand into her back pocket and explained with as much patience as she could muster that she already was grown-up.

Diana waved her hands at Charlotte in a shooting motion. "I toasted the old man out in the garage." She looked over her shoulder and into the mirror at the oily ring on the back of her suit. Grinned at it. "I said a very respectful, 'Thank you, sir!'"

The stylist sprays a fat white puff of mousse into her palm and works it through Charlotte's hair, then steps across the room and crouches in front of a low cupboard, begins to rattle around in the equipment stored there. She growls a cartoon, big cat growl of dissatisfaction. "Errrr, errrr."

Am I going to cry? Charlotte wonders. In the stylist's big mirror, she finds her face is a misshapen pancake, just poured on a very hot griddle, starting to do a little shimmy.

"Errrr." The stylist stands and puts her hands on her hips and calls a sing-song, "Ev-ie, do you have my dryer, darling?"

"Never mind." Charlotte pulls apart the Velcro holding the salon's cape in place around her neck, clambers over the awkward foot rests. "I'll just let it air dry today. I'd rather."

"What?" Crunching sequins, the stylist hurries back, her face showing actual astonishment, as if Charlotte is a patient who has risen from the operating table before being sewn up. "You don't want me to style it?"

"No." She feels like a child, risking adult censure, but she goes on, determined, "I don't think you have the same idea of me that I have."

The stylist sets her hands on her waist, just above her tutu. She begins to laugh. "How do you know what idea of you I have?" the stylist asks.

Charlotte's wallet is leafy with money from her trip, and she takes out more bills for the stylist than are needed for the cut and tax and tip. "Here," she says, "I'm not feeling well. This ought to cover everything."

After she pulls the old glass door closed behind her, they start to laugh. They could have waited longer if they had wanted to make sure that she didn't hear.

In the parking lot, the man in the beige wind breaker still sits on the planter. He smokes a cigarette now. It is Charlotte's policy at least to *try* to say hello to everyone, but the man keeps his head down as she approaches him, and she is shaking, feels full of lead, her feet lead, and she passes him without speaking.

The beige sedan that Charlotte drives is a castoff of Charlotte's father's, given to her two years ago on the proviso that she fly to Iowa to fetch it. When the car gets warm, like now, and the upholstery heats up, she can smell his aftershave. British Sterling.

The car moves like lead as she backs up; then screeches the way it often does when she turns the wheels, but all that goes on too long, and she looks out the passenger window, and finds the neighboring car much closer to her car than any car ever should be. She pulls forward. Parks.

A smooth gouge runs down the side of the neighboring car, like a giant has trailed his finger along the metal. There is, however, no mark on her car.

She looks toward the bungalow, the big window that would be the one next to the stylist's chair. Empty.

She calls to the man on the planter. "Excuse me! This probably sounds like a crazy question, but did I just hit this car?"

He shrugs. "Not that I know of."

She holds her face turned away from the gouge. She thinks: *I'll stand there long enough to allow the stylist or someone else to come out and say if I did something.* The man stands up, then. Has she made him uncomfortable? She gives a weak laugh. She says, "My dad died recently. I get confused."

He takes a set of keys out from the pocket of his jacket and starts across the parking lot, but then he stops and he turns and says, "Well, you know, that's understandable."

(RE) DISCOVERY POET

Alice Anderson

Alice Anderson

THE WATERMARK

3 days after the storm, Main Street Methodist Church, 4 blocks
from the Gulf of Mexico, Ocean Springs, Mississippi

It is almost ten in the morning, and finally I've come
out of the alley, where I dole like contraband to the
residents of Red Cross Shelter #13, out of black plastic

garbage sacks, the entire wardrobe of my three children

and myself. There is, in shelters such as these, a
No Acquisitions policy, so that the displaced cannot
waste too much space along the slick floors with

unnecessary belongings. But I've a house

twenty-seven blocks away, chock full of a terrible, lucky
abundance, untouched by storm surge, by the salty
seep of rising flood, untouched, even, by wind. Folks flip

through the stacks of clean underwear like shoppers

flipping through stacks of dusty albums at a Saturday
morning tag sale. With the clothes it's grab fast and
go, pulling them on over what they already have,

right there in the alley. But the eager girl from

Ann Arbor, with the telltale white T – that bold Red
Cross emblazoned in the middle, ironed creases
at each sleeve, has looked twice out the window

on the alley, so I slam the hatch and go in. We don't need

another incident with an officer, like yesterday. I thought
Billy Gautier, who lost everything, has his whole family
camped out crammed in his station office, might strangle

41

the poor girl. The social hall is nearly untouched.

Yes, the walls are still wet, all the way up to almost
the top. The tiles of the floor lift in patterns, leaving
asbestos shadows on the undersides of mismatched

bedding strewn across the floor. Yes, the splintered

piano keys are wedged into windowsills and the back
wall is a papier-mâché mural with inches of the pulpy grayish
remains of a thousand hymnal pages. There is no longer

a door, now only a way. But the hall is still here. I stand

behind the counter of what used to be the kitchen,
passing out granola bars and bottles of water to
the survivors – the families from the big houses

on East Beach, who will rise up, carried away to family

in the Delta by tomorrow noon, latest. I hand over
apples to single men, wanderers come to Ocean Springs
from New Orleans with the season change, to the frantic

sunburned families from, as we all called them in town

The Complexes – dingy apartment homes right
on the water filled with the working poor, or disabled
elderly, or welfare debutantes with hourly rates, crack

dealers, all Coast Trash living in the *Savanna Luxury Estates*.

They're easy to spot, the ones from the complexes, in
the shade-dappled rusty light from mud-crusted
windows, their feet bare, eyes hollow, as they slink up

to the front of the line, passing through the shadow

of the fallen church steeple out front, pointing
not up now to the heavens, but over, choked
with moss, like a shaggy exit sign pointing west,

commanding everyone GET OUT. They move

slowly, heads down, stringy hair thick with storm water
silt, wearing my dresses, my jeans, a tall man with a black eye
squeezed into my boy's sleeveless New Orleans Saints jersey,

his red belly jutting out between the borders of the jersey

and his rigid, mud-thick bell bottom jeans. And at the way
back tail of the line, there is a girl, a sort of ordinary girl, pretty
in a way you think a pattern of cheap duct tape stuck

to a wall after a makeshift sign has fallen is pretty, found

art, eyes black as midnight, freckles either God-given
skin starlight or simply splattered mud, in her fragile communion
dress edged in Irish lace, Social Security number still scrawled

in Sharpie on the alabaster underside of her arm

in her father's slanted hand. And on her dress: a
meridian, smack dab across the middle of her sunken
chest, right where her frenzied swimming heart nearly

drowned , but was baptized by fire instead, a spare

but graced rebirth. This almost lovely scrappy girl, possibility
in a ravaged dress, catastrophe spelled out in
seed beads and sequins, alive, above the watermark.

Alice Anderson

THE QUIET

Ocean Springs, Mississippi, August 30, 2005, the day after Katrina made landfall.

> *A nutria is an approximately twelve-pound, armadillo-like furry bayou rodent,*
> *the female possessing multiple breasts on her sides so that her young can*
> *suckle while she floats down quiet bayous, inlets, and canals.*

She comes slinking in late for the party, empty-handed and all dolled up
in a soiled taffeta dress. She finds you sleeping, nude on the slab, and licks

with her mossy boozy tongue the length of your grimy thigh. She's
one of those girls who lies down drunk in a big windy swish on

your divan and that's the end of that and you ain't never getting her
out. She comes in after the freight train roar of the storm surge, after

the water with her slapping hips and grand castle of meticulousness
has had her way with it all. She is the water's little sister, not quite as

pretty, but three times as stubborn with something to prove.
                                                    She comes in
quiet, like prayer. She can't make a preacher cuss, can't make him

speak in tongues, but she is the new truth – the word, etched into
every drenched surface, never uttered aloud. She tiptoes in
                                        while the grown-ups

fight, like a pregnant teenager through an evening window, out past
curfew and tipping over the sill. The quiet slaps the hand of snickering

children and smothers the mouths of fucking lovers with her palm. You
cannot escape her. She is obliteration in a see through chemise. When
the quiet comes, she's hungry, and even after she's gobbled up the birds,
their wee petite wings crispy in her teeth, even after she's

sipped the pulp

of every last dragon fly and supped up the oil off every drowned cat, she
still holds a twin set of muddy god-damn-Uncle-Poot-shot-enough-to-

score-a-twelve-pack nutria females under the bathwater, their rubbery
tails knocking suds over the edge, sopping her scabby knees, until they're

quiet, until they float one last time. And then she eats them, too. The

quiet
is satisfied with nothing less than oblivion: she shushes the babies and

stifles the wives. She is a husband's raised hand and the sting that won't
settle on a porcelain cheek. She yanks and twists the royal blue robes up

over the heads and into the mouths of the choir. She is the new hymn,
exalting her praise to destruction. She is your daily chorus, endlessly

repeating. You'll never forget her song. No place to rest in the quiet. She's
the ice box stopped, the leaf blower come to heavenly conclusion. She's

got Michael Chertoff by the shirt collar and she's bound him with violet
feather boas before stuffing him into a FEMA trailer back closet and

turning the lock. She's the opposite of birdsong, enemy of buzz, she's
pulled the tongues from thirty-two miles of lost dogs wandering the coast.

She snakes through the leafless trees and the cracked carcass of what used to be your home. The quiet, she's a breeze - buck naked, with

nothing to strum. She's the moment before the moment, right before the power comes back and the breaker explodes. She's leaking into
every

broken up waterlogged surface of your life, leaking like the breasts of your daughter's best friend's mother. The quiet wasn't there as the
family axed

through the third story rooftop. The quiet doesn't care they held on six hours to a tree. She only showed up the next day, sauntering in to

the room when Baby, their smallest boy, quietly died of water poisoning when no one was looking. The quiet leaks warm milky rivulets on the

mourning mother's borrowed dress. She's there in the eyes of the sister, she's there in the frost of the morgue. No one gets buried in the quiet,

while the earth is too sodden and the mausoleums have been reduced to dusty piles of marble and bone. She's the sadness, the nonsense

lullaby, she's the funeral hush. She saunters by and tosses your *Don't Loot I'll Shoot* sign down, puts your pistol in your mama's lace brassiere.

She is calm and catastrophe, one.
She is calm and catastrophe, both.

She comes in an unspoken promise, that girl, after the surge, and wraps her slight thighs around your hips and she hangs on tight, bucking up

against every bright moment of your devastation. The quiet is your
confirmation. She's set you down on a life of broken glass, and she loves

your bare feet. The quiet comes, wrapping her aching body around you,
her budlike breasts pushing up against your lungs, tickling and
                                                        moistening

the skin of your ear with her terrible, silent tongue. Finally, whispering,
Dance, pretty girl, dance. The quiet is your unrequited lover, come finally

to take you: a gun to your throat, a diamond ring in her mouth. She locks
your thighs in her ghastly grip, and never stops kissing you while
                                                        she fucks.

Alice Anderson

THE WATER
In memory: 238 dead, 67 missing, August 29, 2005.

> *Hurricane Katrina made its final landfall near the state line as just a Category 3 hurricane, but with sustained winds of 120 mph. Katrina's powerful right-front quadrant passed over the west and central Mississippi coast, causing a commanding 27-foot storm surge, which penetrated 6 miles inland in many areas and up to 12 miles inland (maintaining its brutal 27-foot surge) along bays, rivers, inlets, and bayous.*

She comes in quick, after the wind. She comes a towering fortress of
exactitude, skirts gathered up then let loose around her in the terrible,
                                        swirling Fais Do Do.

She is stirred up and she's been drinking since dawn. She comes in with the
darkness but she's not ashamed, nor hiding, nor subtle. She is tall as the
                                        day is

long and her breasts leak with the searching hungry mouths of greedy
little boys always underfoot. The water is wide, her hips slap against
                                        the doorway to your

entire life. She engulfs you like an orgasm that won't ever quit, her wet
                                        excess
going and going and going breathing alive with electricity, like the
                                        sharpness of

a slap on sunburned skin. She rattles the pilings and scoops up the boats,
                                        she is
whoring with the water moccasins and devouring the cats. And the
                                        squirrels and

the rats and the possum and the god-awful-please-shoot-em dollar-a-tail
                                        nutria
we were trying to be rid of in the anyhow. The dead beasts turn in an
                                        ornate

concoction within her and becomes the punctuation in the alphabet of sticks which used to be the buildings of this town. The birds have all flown away. The water is your lover and your end. She is inescapable, sweet as King Cake and three times as festive. Baby Jesus spirals in her roiling destruction
like a

child swaddled in nothing at all. She's kicking it up with confusion, not sure if she's to scratch her watch or wind her ass, but happy to have caused

a commotion. She is the new creation, remaking every surface with her slate gray fate. Her desire thrums like a motorboat's engine on a fine Spring day.

She's a silver tea service guest in every home, she rips the rug from the floors and the leaves from every branch. She's greedy, and pretty, and

loud. When she arrives at the mausoleum she slinks into every last crevice and sucks the dead out with her when she goes.

When the water goes she goes without pause. No time to waste. She rushes back into evening like a train on a switch, a girl

thrown from a high rise, soiled water slipping down a wide open drain. She leaves the beaches littered: deep freezes empty of fish, splintered

hulls of party boats, shards of china and brick, dead bodies ripped nude of their Sunday funeral best, shoes and toys and tires and shovel heads

and lawn mowers, ten thousand formerly frozen rotting chicken carcasses, fat playground elephants up-ended from their rusty

springs, blankets in branches, a vast expanse of Styrofoam
beer coolers upside with no one come to the fete.

She is death or desire, one.
She is death and desire, both.

She comes in and takes you like a lover, swift and fierce and seemingly
devoted and takes all your money (and your children) when she goes.

Andrea Lewis

CRYONIC FREEZE

Julian Loves Adelaide, Part I.

Some call it hoarding; Adelaide calls it art. Adelaide calls it an ever-evolving acquisitional exercise, a six-room palimpsest, a domesti-cosmos. The entry hall narrows to a long intestinal curve lined with stacks of *Time*, *Good Housekeeping*, Walgreen's flyers and the *Abilene Reporter News* skillfully layered and teetering to the ceiling. "I get texture by alternating folded spines and cut pages," Adelaide explains. An effect so stunning that Julian kisses her right there in the newsprint gloom.

The kitchen unfurls with garage-sale finds, from ashtrays to ice skates to an upright piano. "You don't want to mix garage sale with retail," Adelaide says. "It's tacky."

Her bedroom is a mail-order Taj Mahal. Most of the items—over-the-door shoe organizers, drawer dividers, hypoallergenic pillows, 1000-piece jigsaw puzzles, hinoki toothbrush holders and hands-free soap dispensers—are still snug in their original bubble packs. "I love shrink wrap." Adelaide comes up behind Julian and hugs him, pressing her little cone breasts into the middle of his back. "There's something about an impermeable barrier." Her bunk beds hold stalagmites of bright clothing, Technicolor towers of catalogue togs in pomegranate, eggplant, amaranth and pearl.

"Where do you sleep?" Julian asks.

Robert Loves Francine. Francine Wears Red (For Texas Tech).

Robert has spliced his shoelace with staples and he reeks of rose-scented products from the Radisson bathroom. He has come to Dallas to ask Francine for money. Now she's striding toward him, high heels, tight red skirt, red jacket, hair more metallic than he remembers from their days as college lovers. He opens his arms for a hug, but she sticks her hand out, wrist wreathed in charms shaped $, £, ¥, ¢, and €.

"Robert." Only Francine could drench those two syllables with so much subtext. Why doesn't she just say: Your hair's thinner, your eyes are bloodshot, your wife left you, your shoelace is stapled, your account is overdrawn?

"Francine."

Robert distracts himself with coffee-shop minutiae. Francine's plate and its halo of croissant crumbs. Or maybe that's gold. Maybe, without even mentioning money, she is shedding wealth onto the table from her ring-jammed fingers.

"Robert?" she asks. "Do you need money?"

He studies his plate, the two sclerotic boards of bacon, the blob of coagulated eggs. Muffin alveoli clogged with butter. "Yes. Yes, I do need money."

Francine smears strawberry compote onto an open croissant wound. "Well, Teodor's rich," she says. "That's why I married him."

"What does he do?"

"Garbage. Teodor is the lord of Dallas landfills."

Robert pictures their plates scraped into bus trays, leftovers trucked to a landscape of hillocked trash. Crows and seagulls, rats and roaches, stoked on BHA and bromates, nitrites and di-glycerides.

"Just a loan," he says. "I have a job offer."

"Robert, that's excellent." Francine sips coffee and that prehensile upper lip of hers leaves parallel red lines on the cup, a road map into her mouth, and Robert wants her back. He doesn't care about the twenty-two intervening years. He doesn't care about the recent spate of bad luck that began with his whistle-blower report on sodium benzoate and ended with his ex-wife changing the locks. "Where will you work?" Francine asks.

"Texas Cryonics."

Francine has taken out a Coco-Chanel-logo-covered checkbook and a gel pen encrusted with gems. "You left a job as chief chemist for Houston Foods to work with frozen heads?"

Felix, Living History Enactor, Drives to Aurora, Texas.

I always stop at roadside attractions—emporia featuring pecans and pralines, rocks and minerals, fringe and feathers, turquoise and silver, pottery and postcards, placemats, ponchos, beads, greeting cards; or little museums, snake farms, curio stands, wildlife displays, like the one here at Exit 115 off I-20 with its hand-hewn billboard: NATURAL HISTORY OF THE AREA: PANORAMAS AND TABLEAUX. AIR CONDITIONED.

First thing in the door: a taxidermied javelina—a fang-baring, stuffed usherette——with disconcerting blue eyes and a rakish smile, crouching by a WELCOME sign. No admission charged, but a young man stands behind a counter where rubber lizards and Lifesaver mints are for sale, and a Lucite box labeled "Donations" holds a dime and a dollar bill. "Hi. I'm Julian," the young man begins, "and this is my museum." But then a young woman comes through a white door behind him and he turns and all six foot-one-or-two of him draws toward her like a full-body magnet to a full-body ingot of iron. But he stops short of attaching himself to her, and she smiles an I-love-you smile, and the back of his head swells with happiness. She is a vibrant tuning fork of a girl tuned only to this young man, making the very air around them ping and spark, making me put five-dollars in the Lucite box.

NATURAL HISTORY OF THE AREA—its Prairie Dog Village, its Caddo Diorama, its Armadillo Arcade—pales next to these two. They are their own tableau, their own air-conditioning, their own billboard for each other. She wears bright yellow tights, Tony Lama boots and a short, flouncy, horizontally striped black and white skirt with a turquoise tube top around her skinny chest. Her long curly hair—the color of a stack of truck-stop waffles—is tied back with a black chiffon scarf; looped around her neck are a million miles of multi-colored beads. But even this Pollock-painting of a get-up cannot conceal the fact that she is a natural beauty, a scrubbed and beaming captain for the team of Humankind. The young man—Julian—is all corduroy and polyester, horn-rimmed and comb-tracked back to 1959 or '60. "Adelaide," he says, and the word comes out like a red balloon.

She grabs him by the wrist—she has to reach because they still stand an unnatural distance apart even though he leans into her at a dangerous angle, like a tree over water on a spongy bank—and she says, "Lunch is ready."

From The Greek *Kryos*, Meaning Icy Cold.

ROBERT: You don't hear the name Adelaide much these days.

ADELAIDE: I hear it all the time.

ROBERT: Do you know what cryonics is?

ADELAIDE: Cryonics is the low-temperature preservation of humans and animals who can no longer be sustained by contemporary medicine, with the hope that healing and resuscitation may be possible in the future.

ROBERT: You studied up.

ADELAIDE: I need a job.

ROBERT: Do you have experience as a receptionist?

ADELAIDE: Don't we all? Isn't life a process of being receptive to people and experiences and products?

ROBERT: Well, there's filing too.

ADELAIDE: Let's see—the alphabet, right?

ROBERT: Okay.

ADELAIDE: You'll be lucky to get me. I'm currently sifting offers from a Shell Full Service Mini-Mart and a Tony Lama Outlet Store.

ROBERT: Why do you want to work here?

ADELAIDE: To be near my boyfriend. He works one exit down I-20, Exit 115.

ROBERT: What does he do?

ADELAIDE: Taxidermy. Natural history of the area.

Julian Loves Adelaide, Part 2.

Julian's mother—Francine Stephenson Parker Jankowski from Corpus Christi, Texas, now residing, courtesy of waste removal overlord Teodor Jankowski, in the gated Dallas suburb of Purple Sage East, in a house where the doorknobs are disinfected daily and the Steuben glass doo-dads are placed on the hand-crafted oak-burl end tables using a ruler to position them properly, who sometimes throws away clothes she has worn once and who opens the cellophane on a new bar of Lavande de Provence soap every morning because she will not tolerate soap slime and who believes that her Crazy Son has finally found a Nice Girl—wants to meet Adelaide. "Bring her over," Adelaide says.

"Mother," Julian says, "this is Adelaide. Isn't she beautiful?"

Adelaide, knowing that Julian's mother was a cheerleader at Texas Tech and knowing that the Raiders' colors are scarlet and black, has chosen carefully. She wears a black-and-red western shirt with a bucking bronco over the left breast and a red fiesta skirt with so many starched petticoats that it stands out from her waist like a red linoleum countertop.

Moving down the burrow of the entry hall, Francine works to constringe her shoulders, a porcupine-spine-flattening move to keep her clothing from the paper towers and their still-powerful smell of ink. They burst into the living room as if ejected from a tube, and Adelaide says, "Would you like to experience my life story?"

Julian eyes his mother. He understands the overload induced by Adelaide's collectanea, but he's never seen his mother speechless. Is she stunned more by the Silver Lining Photo Wall—a floor-to-ceiling, ten-foot-wide corkboard completely collaged in snapshots—or by the Kiddy Cupboard—glass-fronted shelves with clothes, coloring books and report cards from every phase of Adelaide's early life? Adelaide narrates the photo display ("Here I am on the Atlas ICBM Highway with my step-dad Earl."), points out her favorite baby clothes ("Superwoman pajamas. I thought I could fly!"), and shows off some of her better report cards ("A's in spelling, tennis and chemistry").

When his Mother's eyes take on the unfocused opacity of a bad elk-head mount he once saw in an old hunting lodge, Julian decides they should retire to the shade of the Sculpture Garden, where Adelaide appears with a turquoise teapot and an alphabetized assortment of teabags. Julian is pleased when his mother and Adelaide find one thing in common (besides him): a love of cellophane.

Felix, Living History Enactor, Contemplates His Future.

My job this summer in Aurora, Texas, is to portray Ezekiel Goff, one of the Texas pioneers who in 1897 found a wrecked spaceship that had collided with a windmill. Nearby they found the corpse of the alien who apparently had piloted the ship. It was a child-sized, wizened cadaver, freeze-dried as if by lightning, with wide-set eyes, large feet, and a forehead knurled like a delicata squash. (One sketch is extant.) The residents of Aurora at that time—forty or fifty souls—convened to determine whether the Little Creature, as they came to call it, could be interred in a Christian cemetery, given that the poor thing (they assumed) had been neither baptized nor shriven.

Ezekiel Goff (my character) is pro-Christian burial, which seems the more sympathetic position, but we have little control over which part we're given. I could just as easily have played Burrell Bandy, who wanted the Little Creature burned on a pyre to see if incubi would fly out. My one line is "God loves all the creatures of our universe." Being a professional, I overlook my agnosticism and give it the conviction of a Congregational minister.

The re-enactment features a funeral procession—pine box borne aloft—in the Aurora Cemetery, where the Little Creature is in fact still buried. This ceremony is laden with reverence for the unknown. Reminds me of 18th-century astronomers who, when they discovered moons orbiting other planets, believed it meant the planets were inhabited; because why would God put a moon around a planet except for the enjoyment of the humans viewing it in their sky? Clearly Ezekiel Goff bought the idea of a human-like creature piloting a spacecraft.

Other summers, I have played a Comanche, a 1920's wildcatter, a settler who gets scalped, Joseph Glidden (the inventor of barbed wire), and an "Early Indian" confronting a wooly mammoth with a spear-point lance. The latter was not historically accurate, but I was young and looked good in a loincloth.

Alas, mine is a dying art. Attendance is down. Nobody cares about history. I'm losing jobs to cheap labor—bored kids from Texas Tech who smoke dope behind the fake barns. I'm getting too old to play bare-chested Comanches. I may open my own attraction, or team up with someone else—Cascade Caverns or The Devil's Rope Museum.

The End Of The World As We Know It.

Robert discovers that most of the Winfield house is underground. Entry is via a doorway in a rock dome, which he reaches after being beeped through three concentric rings of electric fence, each with a barbed-wired gate, video camera, and intercom console. Sarah Winfield, cropped salt-and-pepper hair, camo tank top, and prairie-woman denim skirt, greets Robert under the rock dome, holding Eva, her German shepherd, on a short tether. They wind down a long, dim hallway, stacked on either side with boxes labeled NONCORROSIVELY PRIMED AMMUNITION and TEXTURED VEGETABLE PROTEIN, into a low-ceilinged room furnished with metal folding chairs and a metal folding table.

Sarah shows off her new 9-tray Excalibur food dehydrator. "All your fruits, your apples, your plums," she pulls out one sparkling, empty drawer after another, "you plop 'em in here and *wall-lah*, you get dried stuff that lasts for months."

And you want to be similarly preserved? But he has learned to let the clients have their little fanfaronade.

Sarah shoots Robert a slit-eyed glance and speaks in acronymese: "TEO-TWAW-KI."

He nods sagely. *The end of the world as we know it.* He had thought cryonics work would be all cancer patients and kidney failures, but here in Texas, it's mostly survivalists. "Grim times coming," he says.

Sarah leans in, eager now to commune with a cohort. "Would you like to see some body armor?" she asks.

Robert smiles. "Let's talk cryonics."

Back at the office, Adelaide is spritzing her computer screen with Windex when Robert bursts in, brandishing night-vision binoculars—Sarah's idea of a gift—and waving a check for a hefty down payment on five future frozen corpses. "Lesbian couple, two kids and a dog. They're oil millionaires."

Adelaide beams. "Way to go."

"Do you want these?" He scopes an infrared-illuminated Adelaide for a moment, then drops the binocs on her desk.

Everybody Skate!

Adelaide rolls like a pro in her new lavender Firestar Derby skates, her hair flowing back, her white vinyl miniskirt twitching with every synthesized beat from the electric organ's double-time rendition of "Everybody Wants To Rule the World." Julian does what he can to keep up, just happy to be there under the vaulted wooden ceiling of The 18-Wheeler I-20 Roller Rink, with its smells of rental-skate disinfectant and fresh hot dog buns, its old gel lights, its single mirrored ball turning like a lonely asteroid in the Texas night. Herds of toddlers sprawl and fall all over the rink like baby springboks taking their first steps, knobby knees knocking. Julian waits for the slow songs, like "Sweet Dreams" and "Always on My Mind," when he can skate side by side with Adelaide, holding crossed hands, his whole body twanging with the intimate unison of push and glide.

They sit out the Sixty-and-Over Skate in the snack bar crunching Sno-Cones and gazing at one another. "Will you marry me?" Julian asks, lips purple with grape syrup.

Adelaide's cheeks turn as pink as her raspberry ice. "Julian, do you mean it?"

"With all my heart."

"But what about your mother?" Adelaide squishes her cone to siphon syrup to the brim. "She doesn't like me."

"Mother's just miserable," Julian says. "Teodor is leaving her."

An upbeat "Blue Velvet" swells from the Hammond organ. The sixty-and-over crowd comes puffing into the snack bar, ordering coffees and ice cream sandwiches.

Adelaide says, "Let's skate."

Felix, Living History Enactor, Despairs.

You're at a Shell Full-Service Mini-Mart at Exit 116 on I-20, where oil rigs bob their heads like maniacal earth-nursing babies, and you are pumping gas, thinking: Nice trick, Earth: burying the oil down there and getting us addicted as surely as if it were crack cocaine or Starbucks coffee, so that we are compelled to suck it all back out come hell or high water—both of which, we figure, *are* coming—while we wage a few wars to assure it's us-not-them who swallow the last few drops after we toss a few gigatons of previously-earth-bound carbon into the air as casually as confetti at a wedding and let the polar bears take the heat for our heedlessness, even though we're dying anyway, like strung-out junkies in a snowdrift. Yet we are pumping gas. Why?

Because we are on the road. Because this drive to drive, this urge to move, to saddle up the camel and see what's over the next sand dune is entwined with our mitochondrial DNA, but it's all gone awry. We came down from the trees, up from the grasslands, and into an SUV. We drove. We motored. We headed for that Texas horizon, flat as the flat-line on a heart monitor, straight to the brink of extinction, all the while pumping gas. You planned it, Earth, didn't you? Now you're just showing off. You're teasing us, with the Shell brachiopod up there on the sign, while the cheetahs dematerialize and the Maldives take their final dive.

But we are driving, driving across this state, this Texas—which is a word meaning "friends" or "allies" in Caddo, which is a language of the Southern Plains spoken by the Caddo Nation, a language with three short vowels, three long vowels, and a few fricatives and plosives, a perfectly good language, although we'll never hear it because our beloved ancestors wiped out all the Caddo speakers in their mitochondrial dash to the Pacific Ocean to see if it had any oil.

Fight For The Scarlet And Black.

The mailbox is a modified Tonka toy garbage truck and the doorbell plays the Texas Tech fight song.

"Robert?" Francine answers wearing an old Raiders football jersey and rabbit-fur mules. "What are you doing here?"

"I brought you a check." He pulls his wallet from his Levis and five forlorn movie stubs fall out with it. "The money I owe you."

"Teodor's leaving me." Her face goes from perfect derma-braded planes to a squished spigot of tears. "He's leaving me for a bacterial engineer," she wails. "Some gal from India who does environmental cleanup."

Robert anchors his check under the closest crystal statuette, a polar bear on an ice floe, and says, "Would it be bad timing to tell you I love you?"

Francine dabs her eyes with her jersey sleeve. "And my son Julian is getting married."

"Francine, I want you back. I've never loved anyone as I love you." He grabs her arm over the suede 17 on her other sleeve.

"I think his girlfriend might be crazy," Francine says. "Although she seems nice. Her name's Adelaide."

"Adelaide? That's my receptionist's name."

"I'm jealous. Can you believe it?" Francine stomps one mule soundlessly on the deep-pile carpet. "Jealous that my son found love and I can't."

"But *I* love you, Francine." He caresses the 17. "I love you more than ever."

"In fact, I'm *so* mad at Julian," Francine says, "I might cut off the funding for his stupid little museum."

Cartilage pops as Robert drops to one knee. "Francine, will you marry me?"

She looks at his upturned face. "Will I what?"

From The Greek *Taxis* Meaning Movement And *Derma* Meaning Skin, Or Julian Loves Adelaide, Part 3.

Before the wedding, Julian wants to finish two coyotes. He breaks the bubble wrap on a new jawset and tongue assembly and takes one of the skins out of the freezer. He opens a drawer of glass eyes and studies them, his mind drifting as always to Adelaide, forward to their future and backward to making love in a kaleidoscopic sea of thrift shop coats or in the bathtub or in the Sculpture Garden, where they lie some nights on quilts under a starry Texas sky framed by Adelaide's fantasy animals welded from oil drums.

Julian works the clay on the coyote underform, whistling "Everybody Wants To Rule The World" through his teeth and barely noticing the passage of time. He is surprised to look up at six o'clock and see Adelaide coming in from work. "Epoxy," she smiles. "That smell turns me on."

"From our first time," Julian remembers.

"That day I made lunch and that nice older man was here." Adelaide moves scalpels, scrapers, and fungicidal sealants to one corner of the table and tugs off her Tony Lama boots.

"He left five dollars," Julian remembers, unbuttoning his shirt. "His name was Felix."

Adelaide wriggles out of her poodle skirt and climbs onto the table.

"I don't have any impermeable barriers," Julian warns.

Afterward, while Julian files down the points on the jawset assembly and Adelaide gets dressed, she says, "Hey. I discovered that my boss knows your mother."

Felix, Living History Enactor, Regains His Faith In Humankind.

After the alien-funeral pioneer Ezekiel Goff went wherever alien-funeral pioneers go in the off-season, putting me out of a job, and after I burned up more petroleum distillates wondering what to do and where to go next, and after I returned like a magnet to Exit 115 and NATURAL HISTORY OF THE AREA: PANORAMAS AND TABLEAUX, AIR CONDITIONED and accidentally arrived on the day of the double wedding—Julian to Adelaide and Robert to Francine—and after I teamed up with Julian to create *Living* and Natural History of the Area with a fresh infusion of cash from Francine and her fourth husband, the Cryonics Czar of Central Texas, only then did I buy an electric car and become godfather to Clementine, Julian and Adelaide's baby girl, who has already played a Caddo infant in a Living Tableau of Bygone Tribes, and who reminds me daily, sitting in her highchair in her Superwoman pajamas watching Julian stretch a skin or Adelaide slit the shrink wrap on a new toddler toy, that even if the world does not remain the world as we know it or the world as we want it, there will always be children.

Clementine Stephenson Narrates The Silver Lining Wall In Her Dorm Room Prior To Graduation From Texas Tech, 2026.

"Some of my report cards:

> Biological Engineering 402: A
> Cryonics 301: A
> Genetics 331: A
> Synchronous Roller Skating: B
> Caddo Language Studies: A

"A photo of me and my parents and grandparents in front of the famous coyote display in the lobby of Texas Cryonics...

"A photo of me and my godfather Felix and my little brother Ezekiel in front of a Caddo sacred mound in Alto, Texas. The Caddo are making a comeback. They are wonderful people. They have a harvest ritual called a busk, where they bring in the crops and share so that everyone has enough food for winter."

TR Hummer

UNMANNED

Wood columns, verandah, a fanlight.
      Wicker. Ferns. A pile of bones
Next to the dog's bed radiates twilight.
      In the curdling sky, shadows drone
Their numinous presence and zero in.
      Oak planks sawed by prisoners
Warp infinitesimally toward the pure
      condition of dust. All possible pleasure
Has been accounted for. Down the street,
      In every window, disembodied lights appear,
And an X of blood targets every door.

TR Hummer
THE INQUISITION

Along the endless hallway (can infinity be concrete?
      these walls are concrete block) leaning on a walker,
Demanding the worn-out knee (now refitted with steel
      from a cruel dimension not of bone and blood)
To drag the body with it, all this motion a tribute
      to the pure will to Be: like that Cathar spared
His right eye by the Inquisitor so that he might lead
      the other 99 less lucky over the lovely landscape
Of the summer-struck Midi, under the all-seeing, indifferent
      gaze of God, beyond, to the idea of home.

TR Hummer

THE GREAT WATER

The Oracle throws her yarrow stalks. Where they fall
       is defined as Fate. Why not? When the drunk
Truck driver hits a bridge abutment and levitates
       through his own windshield, that portal
Of vision, his load of logs flies too. If he wakes
       barely injured, a chaos of stripped pine boles
Around him, does he survive because he's blessed?
       Divine Providence, he says. Now he lives
Another life. He speaks in tongues. *Thunder*
       under the lake: the Oracle casts her runes.
The superior one at nightfall re-enters the Book of Changes.

TR Hummer

THE END OF RELIGION

Cursed are the galvanized, for rust
      is the ecstasy of entropy.
Cursed are the bleak, for theirs
      Is the wreckage of vision.
Two prophets walk into a bar: *What's*
      it gonna be? Two Buddhists
Walk into the void: *One with everything.*

David-Matthew Barnes
LOOKING FOR HOMER

On a summer train bound for Athens, I'm forcing conversation,
patriotism on strangers, validating everything they've ever heard
about self-absorbed Americans. For once, I'm finally someone's truth.
You are the soldier, the man from Kosovo Polje. You buy me a Coke.
I crave you, one kiss. You make my journey your own, postpone home, hope
to find a new battlefield in me. I'm not yet weary from the war.

We sleep in a bed for the first time in a week, on the third story of Hotel Olympus,
inhaling the piss-sweet stench of Omonia Square. We dream of soldiers, babies,
Belgrade and war, the sunny concaves of a California shore. At dawn we drink
Orange Fantas, change my Lincolns for Drachmas, catch a subway to Piraeus,
board a ship - the Aegeon. My legs, feet are sunburned as we careen, circle
around the Cyclades, looking for Homer, the pulse of a place called Ios.

There, you promise me I shall drown in deep love. I don't look back, high
dive into your arms. At midnight on Mylopotas Beach, I taste the wet tip
of salty waves when your body shudders on top of mine. You – sweet,
breathless, begging me "Don't let go" in broken English. I lick sadness
from your skin, choke back the poet's words: "Men grow tired
of sleep, love, singing, and dancing sooner than war."

Later, when the season of the tourist has come and gone, I, too, become
something no one can ever count on when I fall apart on my twentieth
birthday in a bathroom stall after watching my boss and his brother break
the knee caps of a British boy in the back room of the bar. At dawn, I board
a helicopter; I'm evacuated when shots are fired in the Gulf. I lift off
from the island without *good bye*, so you can become the one true love

I left behind.

Charles Atkinson

QUAKER WITNESS

Tom Fox (1951-2006), Christian Peacemaker Team

Brought himself to Baghdad's
    hell—door to door,
        offering to talk and listen.
        While we sleep they bomb . . .
    our women . . . caress the rubble . . .
fragments of our children . . .

He would "Do unto others . . ."
    Imagine. Prayed for them all.
        Taken hostage, he
        fingered his rusted chains—
    a rosary, a *sebha*—breathing
each captor's name.

They say that under sand
    a river courses, inviting
        life wherever it rises;
        though it's near the surface,
    a person cannot tap it
till he casts no shadow.

Who understands the desperate?
    Drove him past the outskirts,
        discarded his corpse in a ditch.
        Later, children claimed
    the gutter sprouted reeds.
Then came the rain.

Charles Atkinson

PARADISE ON EARTH

Rainbow Over the Potala Palace, Lhasa
—Galen Rowell photograph (1981)

The first time I saw it, I wept: brooding mountains,
    huge sky, both gun-metal gray.
        A rainbow arcs down to a tiny structure,
            the Cosmos fingering a trifle—a gleaming monastery
    harboring 1400 years of wisdom,
chosen—and dwarfed—by a band of colored light.

            *

Thirty years later, I'm there, the Palace wall
    colossal in early sun. There's not enough
        air in the world at 13,000 feet.
            Who can climb another 14 stories?
    Strings of Tibetan pilgrims file past:
robust parents hoist swaddled infants,

older children skitter ahead, grandfathers
    smoke and hawk, grandmothers bend double
        as if examining each paving stone.
            No one breaks stride. They trot to the gate, past
    pods of soldiers slung with black machine guns.
My temples pound; I plod into line, and pant.

Stairs, ramps, stairs; pilgrims stream by—
    hearty and feeble—spinning prayer wheels,
        chanting, not missing a breath. How can
            colors be so tactile! Shawls, blue and
    purple, radiate heat as they climb,
red and yellow sashes chime in the skull.

*

Shrine, stupa, statue, each more lavish—
    encrusted in kilos of gold, rubies, emeralds,
        diamonds in thousands, draped with pilgrims' scarves,
            swathed in the cloying sweet of yak-butter lamps.
    Bodies pushing gently from behind
to view an icon, praying, moving on.

Three-steps-and-a-full-prostration: how many days
    have they spent face-down in the dust? From their presence,
        hushed, this must be the heart of the kingdom:
            Chamber of Eternal Life—the Dalai Lama's
    vacant study. Surely he'll return
to raise them above the fickle tide of empire.

*

Folded away, surviving wisdom sutras,
    handed down the centuries—on palm leaves,
        skins, cloth, paper. Chanted once
            in great halls by 30,000 monks,
    in private now by a skeleton crew dressed like
janitors in jumpsuits, sweeping trash.

They seem indifferent to the glitter shops,
    the tawdry markets engulfing the city below,
        the net cast over them by hard boy-soldiers,
            live ammo on every street corner.
    Here to gather at the seat of an ancient faith,
cleave to the temperate, durable Middle Way.

*

Maybe Galen Rowell got it right:
    plant your camera far across the valley,
        wait for a storm, a once-in-a-lifetime rainbow,
            shoot with a very long lens. At this remove,
    the story's simple: no pilgrims, no army, no grief—
just a yearning for paradise on earth.

2012 LORIAN HEMINGWAY SHORT STORY COMPETITION FIRST-PLACE WINNER

Amelia Skinner Saint

SHIP FULL OF BEASTS

It's morning, but still dark out. Get up and go to the bathroom. The toilet is plugged up with shit and paper and what looks like a smashed up taco. Someone barfed in the sink. Piss in the tub. Don't brush your teeth. Look out the front window. The car that pulled up last night is gone, so go into your mom's room and take five bucks from her purse. Don't bother being quiet, she's at the bottom of the ocean; a cannon couldn't wake her.

Don't wait for the bus. Just walk to school. Let the cold air invade your body, let it fight with the heat of your lungs. Your lungs always win. This is good. This is your first fight of the day and you will win it.

Do you see Barry Basker? He's hiding behind a bush, squatting like a toad, waiting for you to pass by. Don't let him get away with that. Stop. Look to make sure no one is around, then piss into the bush. You can only squeeze a few drops, but it's enough. Barry yelps and stumbles out of his hiding place.

Say: Oh, gosh, Barry. I didn't see you there. I didn't get any on you, did I? I think there's some on your pants. Come here and let me see.

He shakes his head, says he doesn't see anything.

Insist.

Say: No, it's there. I definitely pissed on you. You'd better come here. Come and let me take a look.

He shuffles over like he's got cinder block shoes, but he comes. This is the good part. When he shows you that he'll do something that he doesn't want to do. He would do more. The art of it is in knowing exactly how much more.

Say: Oh, Barry. Those pants are gonna have to come off. Give them here. I've got a pair in my backpack you can wear.

He says: No. It's fine.

Say: I feel terrible about pissing on you, Barry. Really. Let me take them home and wash them for you.

Put your hand on his shoulder. This will make him wince. Wait for that to pass. Wait for him to get used to the feeling of your hand on

69

him. Wait for him to think that maybe you are just being nice, maybe nothing will happen. Then squeeze. Dig your thumb into the hollow above his collarbone. Try to get your fingers and thumb to touch. He struggles, but he can't get away. Squeeze until he falls down. Until he starts to cry.

Say: Oh, gosh, Barry. Now you've got dirt on them too. You'd better let me take those pants. I feel just awful about you getting them all dirty.

He won't get up. He kicks off his shoes, loosens his belt, slips his jeans down over his slender legs. Look at his legs, covered in fine, blond hairs, like a girl's. Go ahead and laugh. It's funny.

Ball up the pants and stuff them into your backpack. Turn and walk away. Don't embarrass him by speaking to him while he's crying.

Go to school. You're early, but don't go inside. If you have too much time to spend hanging around in the hallways before first period, everyone will just expect you to do something. Don't gratify them. You aren't a trained ape. You are a beast. Lay low, save your strength. You're tired from the go-round with Barry. You should be; it was inspired. Rest.

In second period, Angie Oliver sits behind you because she's late and that is the last open seat. She whispers to Emily Bollinger that you stink. You probably do. Pretend you don't hear her. At morning break, go and find her. She's by the candy machines. Snatch the Skittles from her hand, spit in them, and hand them back to her. Keep walking. Don't look at her face; that would ruin it.

You have your mom's money, so buy lunch from the vending machine. Take a bag of Doritos and make the rounds. Don't try to sit with anyone. James Avery walks past like he doesn't even see you. Trip him and make him spill his water. But that is hardly sporting. He's flimsy, lispy, probably queer. He's too easy for you.

Notice the way everyone guards themselves when you come near. They grip their trays tighter, turn their genitals away, avoid sipping their chocolate milk until you have passed. Do you feel it? This is what power is. You move people like the moon moves the tides. Go back to the vending machine. Don't get in line, just lean against the side and watch everyone slyly palm their candy bars and slip their packs of gum up their sleeves. They're magicians, but the thing they really want to disappear is you.

Here is Fat Brandon Wattley. He gets a Twix and does a clumsy pick-and-roll move to the other side of the Coke machine line. Follow him. Catch up with him by the freshman tables.

Say: Hey, Brandon. I'm worried about you, man. We're learning about diabetes in Health Sci, and I'm pretty sure you've got it.

Look around. Make sure people are listening. Humiliation only works if people are listening. If a fat kid falls in the forest, and there's no one there to laugh at him, does he cry?

Say: I'm serious, Brandon. I want to help you with your problem. Pinch his conical boy-breast.

Say: My great-uncle had diabetes and one day his foot fell off. Just dropped right off like a dead leaf. How's your foot feeling, Brandon?

Stomp on his foot. Grind your heel until you feel the toes spreading apart inside his Converse. He hands you the Twix. Stand in front of him and eat it. Watch him rub his foot and cry. Savor his tears like chocolate.

In fifth period, the counselor comes to Geometry class. She's pointing at you with her nose while she whispers to the teacher. The teacher tells you to go with her; he tells you to take your things. Fat Brandon Wattley or Prepubescent Barry Basker has probably run and told on you. Adopt the face: eyes wide, mouth slightly agape, chin tucked in. The what-are-you-asking-me-for face.

But the counselor, with her mouth puckered up and make-up caked in all of the creases, isn't giving up anything. She's making chit-chat as the two of you walk to her office.

How do you like Geometry? I was never any good at proofs, myself. Do you think you might like to study something like that when you get to college?

Slow down. Look at her, so she knows that she's done something wrong. There is no when-you-get-to-college for you. It is supposed to be part of her oath as a school counselor to never remind you that you're too poor and too mean and too low in the social order to go to college. She shuts up and keeps her eyes on her shoes as they clip-clop the rest of the way to her office.

Inside, there are two women in uniforms with their backs to the window and their hats held tight against their stomachs. Don't act surprised. Dont act afraid. One is the bitch school resource officer. She greets you like an old friend. Smile. Be cordial. The other one is a black woman. Smile at her too. Remember, you haven't done anything wrong. They can't arrest you a titty-twister. Maintain your innocent face.

The counselor asks you to sit down. They will expect you to sit in the chair closest to the door. Sit in the one closest to the cops. Show them you are not afraid of them.

The counselor sits down at her desk. The cops stay standing. They're trying to make you feel small.

Resource cop says: William, when did you last see your mother?

Relax. You aren't in trouble. It's just your mom.

She says: Did you see her this morning before school?

Give details. Real memories have details.

Say: Yes, Ma'am. I saw her at breakfast. We had waffles, with strawberries and chocolate syrup.

She says: Oh? So what time was that?

Be exact. Cops love exactitude.

Say: Seven thirty. Before the bus came.

She says: Oh.

The black cop says: Was there anyone else at your house this morning? At breakfast?

She says *breakfast* like it's a made-up meal. Like only wizards and Australians eat breakfast. Ignore that.

Say: No, Ma'am. Just me and Mom.

She says: And last night? Was there anyone else at your house last night?

Say: No, Ma'am. Me and Mom made tacos—we make tacos every Thursday—then we watched *Clash of the Titans* on TV, then we worked on my homework, then we went to bed.

Resource cop says: Hey, I love that movie. It's my favorite. But was it on last night? Or was it maybe another night you're thinking of? Because I watch it every time it's on. I never miss it.

She's trying to trip you up. She thinks she's smarter than you. She isn't.

Say: Oh, no, actually it wasn't on TV. We have it on video.

She says: Oh.

The Black cop says: Are you sure no one else was there? Do you think someone could have come after you went to bed?

She's getting at something. Circling all around it. Your mom did something to the guy who was there last night, the one who shit tacos and puked in the sink. She'll say she never touched him, then who does that leave? They'll think you did it, whatever it is. They'll lock you up for rolling him or stabbing him or biting his dick off. They'll peg you for a jealous little Oedipus. Don't let them.

Say: Well, actually, now that you mention it, I think someone did come after I was in bed.

She says: Uh hm. Did you hear anything? After he—this person—came to your house?

She's looking at you like she's trying to read a map that's tattooed inside your eyeball. Be careful.

Say: Well, I think I heard my mom yelling. I guess maybe she was mad at the guy over something.

She says: What did your mom say? Do you remember?

The counselor clears her throat and spreads her fingers out on her desk. She's looking at her fingers, not you, not the cops.

She says: Excuse me, but aren't either of you going to tell him? I mean, how long can this go on?

The resource cop kneels down next to your chair and puts her hand on your arm. It feels nice, but don't let on.

She says: William, your mother didn't show up for work today, and her boss, he went by your house to check on her. He's the one who called us.

She's squeezing your arm, but not like she's trying to hurt you, more like she's trying to hold onto you.

She says: William, your mother passed away. Her boss found her there in her bed.

She stops talking. She's just looking at you now. She is looking for tears, but she won't find them.

She says: We've been in your house, William. Your mother—she wasn't up making waffles this morning.

The black cop lays a hand on her shoulder and shakes her head. The resource cop gets quiet. She is still holding onto your arm, looking at you, waiting for something to bust. Like a ship run aground with a hull full of salt water. Like she is going to catch all the pieces and hold you together. But she isn't. You aren't full of salt water.

A long time ago, your mother told you that people were all just ships on the ocean, and some of them had captains who knew the way, but some just put up their sails and let the wind take them where it would. She said she was one of those without a captain, drifting in the wind. But you—you had a captain, one with the tools and maps to get someplace. You just had to let your captain steer the ship.

She didn't know what your cargo was. Down in the belly of your ship were rows and rows of wild beasts in their crates. And every time the sea got rough, a crate would burst open and one of the beasts would get loose. She didn't know that a long time ago, the last beast was set free, and one by one, we ate the crew, ate the captain, shit on his maps.

There is no salt water inside you. You are a ship full of beasts drifting on the ocean. You are a ship full of beasts waiting for something to crash into.

Pamela Stewart

TRYING TO FINISH THE NEXT SENTENCE

I turned my head and a bird flew out of my left eye —

That's the kind of day it was, the sun
a red bullet in the hazed-up sky.

The mouse in the field, the mouse
in the skirting board are one truth of life on earth.

I watched the frenzied bantams in their coop
tear up a wandering toad.

Why not just keep walking, I thought,

and learn the sun like a brother
and how to keep the bird from the bullet hole.

Pamela Stewart

I AM A WOMAN TIRED OF WAR

I've been captured by a city which scorns me as an occupant.
War has fingers tiny enough to peel the leaf from its veins.

See that child with no right foot?
The sick doctor is the only one left with two hands.

It used to be that a large sturdy leaf could act as an extra hand.
War breeds a wickedness of imagination.

My words, pecked off the ground by the beaks of translation,
can't begin to tell you . . . .

Pamela Stewart

ALMOST SINGING

Under her breath, she rummages for Christmas.
She pauses to watch the snow and thinks of sin and its wolf prints
on the slope back down to the barn. But that was then —
yes, there's always *then* and *now* and the snowscapes of in-between.
Her breath catches. Never bury a child far from the house. Smoothing
that red wool stocking stretched at the toe, she holds it to her cheek.
Never bury a child where she can't hear you singing.

Pamela Stewart
KEPT GOING

I saw a tattered hemlock
shift her weight. It took
two, maybe three, moments
in the still, snow-ladened air.

Just past Sam's barn, up
that slope where the collie waits,
it happened again,
Like a wave, a larger tree arched

then twisted before it settled.
My pulse quickened
then slowed. I walked, stopped,
Ok I said. Kept going.

Devreaux Baker

WE SHOW EACH OTHER OUR SCARS

We show each other our scars, *think* Krakow at dusk
winter in the yard, lights like globes of fire
trapped in distant buildings, heat bundled in hands

Think the train through Yugoslavia, how the guards
pulled you off at checkpoint, guns slung across their chests

We show each other our scars, *think* the world as lover or
first love, first sex, the heat, the mouth. Years later,
longing mistaken for thirst

We show each other our scars, the clock hands move forward
in increments, time branded on our features, our features
precise mirrors of our mothers or grandmothers;

mine in babushka, overalls, hoeing in the garden,
yours more distant, a dream in quilted coats moving through
your yard. We show each other our scars, *think* distant lands,
filled with the porcelain faces of rivers broken into pieces by fish
against our legs

We are wading across with canvas packs on our backs
We show each other our scars, the world may stop spinning
sometime in the future may speak to us in a language
we finally understand but by then it will be too late

Somewhere there are two women lifting their shirts saying
my scar is on my left breast just over my heart
small smudge, the surgeon left behind this one
shadow trace like eucalyptus leaves at dusk or

mine is on the right breast, hooked under and curving
like a pavilion rooftop, like a smiling moon
a gardenia leaf floating in the pond of my body
moonlight ripples my water

We are standing in the world knee deep, chest deep
treading this flow that sounds like twigs
breaking against our windows

Together the world is standing in us, asking if we are ready,
do we want more, what can we bear to carry
what can we leave behind

Devreaux Baker

MOTHER TONGUE

It is my Mother Tongue
that causes me to hum
at the back screen door
when geese fly by

wings and songs
stirring up the air,
the thread that connects
me to the fabric

of my ancestors
standing in my backyard
or crowded around
my kitchen table.

It is my Mother Tongue
celebrating all night long
black dirt or thunder,

playing spoons with crazy beats
or lighting sweet grass
in bundles.

My Mother Tongue
has bare feet
hair like stormy weather
a heart like wild swans
landing in the pond of me.

This is where I find
all the lost tribes
aunts and uncles
rowdy cousins
and great-great
grandmothers.

This is the table
we share at dawn
and dusk. The meal
that breaks open
the bread of silence

so I am no longer
half this, half that,
living in a stranger's
world.

This is my prayer
for the long river
of her body

all her trials
and tribulations

that lived
in the blue mountains
of her birth.

Mornings I ride the bus
I tuck my Mother Tongue
in my pocket,

listen to her soft speech all day
rising out of my clothes,
all the seams and folds
the stitches alive
with her song,

simple words pulling me
in close
to the dark aorta of earth

offering me
sweet medicine
for my soul.

Lawrence Judson Reynolds
MY FATHER'S NECKTIE

That was the summer I should have become a man. 1953. I turned twelve that year, the year my father had a stroke. It was spring.

Thornton and I got off the school bus at the edge of the highway and found the store closed, the door locked, the shades pulled down. A black Chrysler was parked in the driveway. It wasn't a car that belonged to anyone we knew. Something was wrong. Our father never closed the store during the day. Even when he was in his garage working on someone's car, the door was left unlocked, the shades up. If customers came, they knew where to find him. If they were in a hurry, they took what they needed and left money on the counter or a note telling him to put it on their account. That was the way country stores were in my childhood.

We walked around the side of the store to the house. Our mother was waiting. She herded us to the table on the side porch. We put our books on the table and sat down. I put my head back and looked up at the pale blue sky with its thin patches of gauzy clouds. It was a mild day with sudden gusts of wind that had a bite of cold in them. It would be a good day to fly a kite. I didn't have a kite, but that was no problem. I became a kite. I puffed myself up and waited for the next gust of wind to lift me. Then from high above I would look down on the store, the house, the garage, the highway as they grew small and insignificant.

I was waiting to be lifted up when I heard my mother say:

"Your father's had a stroke."

A stroke? I knew what a stroke was. I had seen old people crippled by them. But when I heard the word come from my mother's lips that day all I could think of was the smooth motion of a hand stroking cat's fur. My father? A stroke? In my mind's eye I saw a hand caressing my father's head. There is a bald spot on the very top. The fingers are moving toward it. The hand thinks it is petting a cat. It is not expecting the slick, bald spot. The hand is in for a big surprise. I grin at my brother, but suddenly I'm aware of my brother's countenance. He's not smiling. He's looking at my mother. They seemed to share a sense of shock, sorrow and determination while I am caught with an inappropriate grin on my face.

I hid my mouth with my hand as our mother gave us our instructions. We were not to come in the house until she called us and we were to be very quiet. We could work on our homework on the porch. I could do my usual chores and Thornton could feed the Cantons' livestock as usual. Supper would be late. She would call when it was ready. She said nothing about father's condition other than to say he was "resting" and a doctor from Lynchburg was with him. Then she went back inside.

Thornton opened one of his books and began his homework. I tried to do the same, but my thoughts wandered. I kept thinking about Thornton, about how he had changed in the last three years, since he was twelve and had gone to work on old man Canton's farm next door to us. In some ways I was like him. Everyone commented on how much we looked alike, how polite we were, how quiet and considerate we were. But I knew we were also very different. As children Thornton and I had been a team. He was the serious one. I was the joker, the jester, the rascal — the one that got us into trouble. Thornton was always there to rescue us. It was a natural role for me but now I was beginning to see that there was no place for foolishness in the world of men. Being a man was serious.

As children Thornton and I had dreamed of taming a wild animal and roaming the countryside with it as our companion. We knew it was possible to tame wild animals. One of our neighbors was an old man named Crews. My father said he was shell shocked in the first war. He lived alone in a cabin back in the woods. People said he had all kinds of wild animals living in the cabin with him. We had seen only one of them with our own eyes — a raccoon that perched on Mr. Crews' shoulder when he came to pick up supplies at the store. There was always a sense of excitement when he came walking up the highway with the coon on his shoulder. Even the adults stopped what they were doing and looked. The cars on the highway slowed. Thornton and I were impressed but we were confident we would tame something even more impressive — a mountain lion or a bear.

One evening not long after my father's stroke, Thornton brought home a baby skunk he had found in the Canton's barn. He said nothing about it during supper, but afterwards, he took me outside and led me to the place where he had the skunk caged in a peach basket. We were not ignorant of the nature of skunks and the sickening smell they produce, but we knew that Mr. Crews kept several skunks that were as tame as housecats. People said he knew how to "operate" on them when they were young and render them harmless. Our skunk was just a baby. When the time was right we would take it to Mr. Crews for an operation.

Our immediate concern was finding a hiding place, a place where our mother wouldn't find it. We didn't have to ask — we knew she would not approve. There were two small buildings in back of the house but Thornton thought they were too visible from the kitchen window. He didn't want our mother to become suspicious, seeing us going in and out of one of these buildings everyday. The only building that was suitable was the old barn. It was on the opposite side and away from the house. The barn was father's garage where he worked on cars, trucks, tractors — anything mechanical. It was his natural occupation. Opening the store had been mother's idea. It appealed to her sense of order and cleanliness. For several years after we moved there he devoted himself to running the store but as the years passed it must have become obvious to him that there was no way to make a living operating a country store. Over mother's objections he started working on cars.

He converted part of the tobacco barn into a garage by cutting an opening through the front wall and pouring a concrete slab over part of the dirt floor. With the barn boards he removed to make the opening, he made a sliding door that opened and closed to let cars in and out. From the outside it still looked like a barn, its sides covered with weathered vertical boards, unpainted. The roof was metal, with patches of rust. On the side away from the house was a regular door with an old brass padlock. Father never locked the garage. The lock was something left by the previous owner.

Inside the barn was a vast darkness — in my imagination it was a setting for nightmares. It was open from the dirt floor all the way up to the underside of the roof. Tier poles — on which the tobacco had been hung for curing — laced the darkness at intervals of four feet vertically and horizontally. At ground level, with the side door open, one could see the shapes of things through a muddy darkness, but up above there was an ancient darkness, a darkness that had been imprisoned when the barn was built, an indelible darkness that even the sharp lines of sunlight that knifed through the cracks could not extinguish. Creatures lived in that darkness. Beetles, spiders, wasps, dirt daubers, lizards. Once a dead bat fell on the hood of a car my father was repairing. But snakes were my worst fear. They wrapped themselves around the tier poles and hung down like lengths of rope, at least that's what happened in the stories the old farmers told. As a child Thornton had shared my fear and we avoided the old building but now as he was becoming a man he scoffed at my fear and insisted on keeping the skunk in the barn. Who could feel comfortable in a building where at any moment snakes might rain down on you?

My father had also installed a chain hoist in the old barn. It was attached to a steel beam that rested on two posts about ten feet apart. This mechanical device had a head full of pulleys and wheels through which the chains were wound and guided in such a way that my father, single-handedly, could lift an engine from an automobile. That was the intended use of the hoist. Its other use was at hog killing time when it was used to lift the carcasses of hogs by their hind legs so the blood would drain from their slit throats. Then their bellies were slit and their glistening bowels cascaded down into a washtub.

During that last year before his stroke my father spent more and more time in the old barn — sometimes working late into the night. When my father had renovated the barn he had removed the lowest tier of poles to make space to drive a car inside but in the upper part of the barn the poles had been left in place. A long extension cord was looped around one of these poles. A light bulb with a round metal shade over it was attached to the end of the cord. It dangled about eight feet above the floor, dropping a gloomy circle of light on the concrete slab. The hoist lurked just at the edge of the light, the beam and the posts barely visible so that it seemed to hang from the darkness itself. When I looked at it in the dim light, it looked like a man hanging from a gallows.

My mother's dislike for the old barn was no secret and once my father had converted it to a garage she refused to set foot inside the place. My brother, who had no fear of buildings or anything else scoffed at the idea of snakes falling from the darkness. He decided it was the ideal place to keep the skunk away from mother's critical gaze.

He lifted the padlock and pushed the door open and vanished into the darkness. I waited outside until he found the light and turned it on. The place was littered with parts — engine blocks, transmissions, starters, generators, radiators. I picked my way carefully through them, moving to the open area between the sliding door and the beam where the hoist hung. Thornton searched the perimeter for holes through which the skunk might escape. I waited under the glow of the light bulb until he came back.

"This will do," he said.

He took the basket from me, sat it on the grease-caked floor and removed the lid and I had my first good look at the skunk. It was a beautiful creature, not much bigger than a fist, with a black and white coat that seemed to glow even under the dingy light. It looked up at me with such innocent eyes it was difficult to believe it would someday be able to produce such a disgusting odor.

Thornton had planned well. He had rags, jar tops, water and some table scraps he had taken from the kitchen. We placed the basket on its side, wedged between an engine block and a toolbox, so the skunk could come and go. We put the rags in the basket to make a bed. Just outside the basket on the floor we arranged the jar tops — one with water, one with food.

The animal showed no interest in our preparations. It would not eat or drink and each time we put it in its bed it immediately got up and walked out on the dirty concrete and stood there looking up at us with eyes that seemed much too big for its body. Finally we gave up. When we left it did not attempt to follow us. It just stood there staring, until we cut the light out and closed the door.

I would like to remember that I was a good keeper. I do remember trying to play with it — holding it in my lap like a cat, talking to it, petting it. But it never warmed to this attention. Its big unblinking eyes were always on me but they revealed nothing other than a general wariness of other creatures. As the days passed it seemed little changed from the first day we put it in the garage. I brought water and food on a regular basis, at least at first, but it had no appetite for what I brought. It did not grow, yet it was not starving. It survived with little physical change there in the darkness of the barn among the rusting car parts and the smell of oil and gas.

My father's stroke had dealt a blow to all our lives. He was unable to get out of bed, unable to speak a complete sentence and unable to feed himself. My mother took care of him, ran the store, fixed the meals, kept the house, and washed our clothes. At first she spoke of it as a temporary thing — "until your father gets back on his feet." It was a reasonable expectation. My father was only fifty-six and had always been in good health. Surely he would recover. I remember her saying to someone soon after his stroke: "Maybe it will keep him out of that garage." She seemed cheerful at the prospect. And she might have continued her Herculean effort indefinitely had it not been for a new complication. After two months in bed, hardly moving and seeming little aware of what was going on around him, my father began falling out of bed. It happened several times in the course of a week, always when he was alone. Each time my mother had to call a neighbor to come over and lift him back into his bed.

I remember a Saturday in late May, the last Saturday before my 12th birthday and the end of the school year. It was my last day of childhood freedom. I decided to spend it fishing. I dug the worms at the corner of our pigpen. The two young pigs squealed as I dug, hoping I would bring another bucket of slops. Across the way in a distant field I could see my brother and Mr. Canton and several other men stacking bales of hay on a wagon. It was a fine day, pleasantly warm but not really hot. As I walked behind the garage, it occurred to me that I had not fed the skunk for several days.

I was lifting the padlock from the garage door when I heard my mother call. There was an urgency in her voice that startled me. I left the food scraps and the cup of water I was carrying in the grass and ran back behind the garage.

As I came up to the back of the house she called again. When I rounded the corner she stood in the yard looking down at a bundle of cloth on the ground. At first I thought she had dropped a basket of laundry. Fortunately I didn't smile or say something foolish, for when I got closer I realized that the bundle of clothes was my father. Somehow he had gotten out of bed and made it to the door, opened it and fallen into the yard.

"Where were you?" my mother asked.

"Digging worms."

"Your father has fallen out of bed," she said. That struck me as a curious way of putting it. It was obvious he not fallen from his bed to the yard.

"Is he all right?" I looked down at him. His eyes were closed and he seemed to be peacefully sleeping in the grass.

"Of course he's all right. He just fell . . ." This time she stopped.

An awkward moment followed. I was too old to simply believe what the evidence before me did not support, but too inexperienced to understand why she would not acknowledge my father's strange behavior.

"Where did you think you were going?" my mother said to my father. He was back in his bed again, thanks to a neighbor who happened to stop at the store just as my mother and I struggled to lift him. She ran her hands over his body, feeling his arms, his legs, his ribs, checking for broken bones or blood or bruises but he had survived the fall without a scratch. She pulled the sheet up over his legs and looked at me.

"Someone has to stay with him," she said. She went to the kitchen and brought back a chair and placed it in the corner of the room.

"Sit!" she said.

I thought this was just another chore my mother was giving me. I would sit there for an hour or two and then I would be free. And in another week I would begin the real work that would make me a man. But it was not an hour or a day or a week my mother had in mind. When the summer ended and the crops were harvested and school was ready to open again, I was still sitting in that room.

Half a century has passed since that long ago summer but even now I have but to close my eyes to feel the slow passing of each hour in that hot and airless room, to see my father's lame eye lurching about, to smell the urine in his bed clothes, to hear the hiss of traffic passing on the hot asphalt outside, and to taste the bitter dust that drifted through the open windows from the fields where my brother was doing a man's work.

My brother grew tall and strong that summer. He became a hard worker who kept his mind on what he was doing. He developed a quiet confidence that the older generation of farmers expected and appreciated in a young man. They told my mother that he was a "natural worker" and she was pleased. I saw very little of him. He was always working. In the evenings when he came in from the fields, he helped my mother in the store and by mid-summer he was tending the store alone in the evening so mother could finish her day of work — the washing or cleaning or cooking.

I sat in the same chair, in the same room all day, every day. Often hours passed and I would not see or talk to anyone. Sometimes my mother gave me chores to do, but mostly I did nothing, saw no one, said nothing.

Night crept in like a fog, blurring the familiar objects in the room — the dresser, the chairs, the bed — until my father's face was at last blotted out. Only the window remained, like a movie screen. Outside fireflies blinked in the shadows of the trees. A faint light rippled over the landscape when a car rushed by on the road and the noise of its passing dimmed for a moment the shrill of crickets and tree frogs.

Sometimes when a customer pulled into the driveway of the store a shaft of light lanced into the dark room illuminating my father's face, his eyes wild and frightened like those of a trapped animal.

The failure of the human body is inevitable and equally unpredictable. We know it will happen — but not to us. Not now, not in the midst of life. We do not expect it to happen — at least, not in one's own family. But when it did happen, the additional work it created fell to the women. The people in our community seldom went to the hospital. Nursing homes were not a part of their vocabulary. The care of the halt and the lame fell to the women. Accidents and epidemics, miscarriage and menopause, illness and old age, lunacy and death lurked at the periphery of woman's work. There was hardly a family around Phoebe without a member whose physical or mental health did not place an additional burden on its wives, mothers, sisters, and daughters.

How does one compare chopping tobacco or getting up hay to sitting hour after hour with an invalid? To the men and the soon-to-be-men, working in the hot summer sun the very idea would have been laughable. Of course, invalids had to be cared for but no fool would think of it as the same as hoeing, suckering, or cutting tobacco. They, the men, were glad to help with the sick and the infirm when a strong hand was needed as when my father struggled out of bed and fell and had to be gotten up. They would stop their work if they were summoned and come on the double.

When my mother thanked them for their trouble, they would say: "Oh, no trouble" as if dealing with the sick was nothing. Or they might say: "Glad to get out of the sun for a few minutes" looking at me, or did I only imagine they were, in my clean shorts and shirt, twelve years old, doing nothing but sitting there drinking a glass of cold lemonade while they worked in the fields.

What did they know of the humiliation of spoon-feeding baby food into your own father's mouth, of lighting his cigarettes and holding them to his lips while he smoked, of learning to shave on someone else's face. What did they know of the groans, the coughing fits, the showers of spit, the snot rags, bedpans, enemas, rubber sheets? Had they ever been locked in a hot room and forced to listen to the tortured sleep of a man whose nightmares perhaps provided the only relief from his terrible consciousness? What did they know of how slowly the time passed in that gloomy, airless room?

A chain hoist does not look like a man, not even in a dream. It's not made to lift a man. A hoist is a clever device designed so a man can lift a three hundred pound engine out of a car. But it was a man's face I saw up there in the gloom of my father's garage. A familiar face, though not recognizable, a grotesque figure with a hooked nose and arms — arms as long and limp as chains, rattling and rising disjointedly like the arms of a marionette. The pulleys whirled as the chains sprang to life. I was being lifted. I felt a movement beneath my feet as if the earth itself were being hoisted up into a dark hell. I looked down — the hooked-nosed man has bound my feet. I am strung up like a hog. I am upside down, swinging and twisting. Beneath me, looking up, is a sea of faces. Something drips from my nose... warm... warm and dark. Drip...drip...drip...drip. Then it begins to run, to trickle, to gush...

I open my eyes and see a ripple of light flicker in the room. A car is passing on the highway. Across the room my brother is snoring softly. I am still in a half-dream state, searching the faces for the hooked-nose man, still feeling the gush from my nose. I put my hand to my nose expecting to feel blood but as I drift up out of sleep the gush of blood turned into the unmistakable, repulsive odor of skunk.

I finally went back to sleep. When I got up that morning the odor was still in the air. My brother had already left for another day of work in the fields. When I came into the kitchen my mother was washing Mason jars at the sink. A bushel basket of half runners, freshly picked, sat on the floor. It would be my morning's work to string and snap the beans while I sat watching my father. In the afternoon my mother would can them, working around the customers who came by the store.

"Smells like we had a visitor last night," she said. She sat the last canning jar on the drain board and went to check on my father. I poured a bowl of corn flakes, put milk and sugar on them — but after a couple of spoonfuls, I wasn't hungry anymore.

"He's still asleep," she said when she came back. "You'll have to feed him when he wakes up. It smells even stronger in the bedroom. I hope we don't have a skunk living under the house. When I was a girl we had a family of them living under our house. Something frightened them one night and the house smelled for a week. We had to eat out of doors to get away from it. It made you sick at your stomach just to think of food with that smell in the air. Oh, it was a lot stronger than this. This is nothing but a baby skunk smell."

A baby skunk smell? The phrase startled me. Was my mother saying that baby skunks were able to produce the scent, or was she merely making a size comparison between the two smells?

As soon as I finished breakfast, my mother got me started on the beans. She liked things done her way. Each time she gave me a new chore she insisted on "getting me started." I took the beans back to the bedroom where my father was still sleeping. My mother followed with a clean pot and an old bucket and some newspapers. Just as she finished her demonstration, we heard a customer pulling into the driveway in front of the store. She left and I began processing the beans from left to right just as she had showed me.

The skunk smell in the bedroom was indeed stronger than in the rest of the house. I remained uneasy. I tried to remember the last time I had taken food and water to the garage. It had been a few days, maybe even a week. The trouble was, the skunk never seemed to eat anything I fed it. Scraps of moldy food piled up. It seemed useless to keep on bringing food. It was clearly time to get rid of it. I hoped I hadn't waited too long already.

I thought I felt someone looking at me but when I looked my father's eyes were closed. I was stringing beans as fast as I could and thought I might have a chance to slip out to the garage after I finished the first lap-full if my father didn't wake up.

After my father's stroke my mother had slept in the day bed on the far side of the room. During the day it served as a sofa for the visitors who came to see my father. Although he seldom tried to speak, and when he did it was almost impossible to understand him. There were lots of visitors. On Sunday, the room would sometimes be full of relatives and neighbors. Most of them stood in the corners of the room and talked to each other around my father's bed. The oldest ones or the ones in ill health sat on the day bed or in the chair where I sat all week.

Each visit followed the same pattern. The visitor entered the room and immediately went over to the bed and spoke to my father. Sometimes he would look at them with his good eye while his other eye rolled beneath its drooped lid. At first they would look directly at him as they talked but under his unblinking gaze they soon dropped their eyes and stared at his hands that my mother had folded on top of the bed cover. Their one-sided conversations would go on for as long as the visitor could think of something to say. Then the visitor would pause, look up again into my father's eyes and smile, pat him on the legs, and drift away. My father's gaze never left them until they turned away, but the eye never gave any indication that communication had taken place. I do not know why but it was my impression that my father hated these visits, hated people standing over him, around him, filling up his space.

I looked at him again lying there on his back, his eyes closed. And I knew he wasn't sleeping. He was hiding deep inside himself. It was a trick I'd learned over the year, a clever way to escape confrontation. Of course my father had known the trick before his stroke, but afterwards, lying there day after day, he perfected it to the point that the light beam of his consciousness was compressed by great force of will to a pure hard diamond.

When I finished the first lap-full of beans, I lifted the newspaper and dumped the strings into the bucket. I laid the paper aside and stood up. With the basket, the pot and the bucket surrounding me I had to move my feet carefully to free myself. I did not want to move anything for fear my mother would find her arrangement disordered.

Standing up I suddenly got a stronger whiff of the skunk odor and I knew I had to get out to the garage as soon as possible. I walked over and stood by my father. His eyelids remained closed but I could see the movement of his crippled eye beneath the lid.

"You want some breakfast?" I asked. I was testing. I knew there would be no answer.

The room was silent. The eye continued to move but the lids remained closed. The silence was broken by the sound of a drink delivery truck pulling into the driveway of the store — an abrupt clatter of bottles as the rear wheels dropped from the edge of the pavement. The delivery would keep my mother busy in the store so I wouldn't have to worry about her returning to the bedroom anytime soon.

It was my father I was concerned about. I would like to believe I was a diligent, concerned caregiver during those times I was forced to sit all day in my father's room. I was not. I took every opportunity to deceive my mother and escape from my station. Over the long weeks of that summer, I had studied her daily routine so that I knew when she was likely to check in on my father and me. During those times I was always in my chair. But the other times when I did not expect her to be there, I often slipped out into the backyard and wandered about, daydreaming and doing nothing. It was during my absences that my father attempted his own escapes and would end up helpless on the floor. Each time this happened I had to explain to my mother why I had not stopped him from getting up, why I had not called her sooner. After all, this was my responsibility — to keep him from getting out of bed.

Had he continued to make these escapes, I would have had no choice but to stay with him every minute, but after a couple of close calls, he stopped trying to go wherever it was he wanted to go and I was free to slip out without fear of coming back and finding him on the floor.

I often felt he was telling me to leave. He did this by closing his eyes and feigning sleep, just as he was doing now. I would like to believe he was sympathetic to my boredom and was kindly giving me his permission to go out and play. But that was not the feeling I got. He had his own reasons for wanting me out of there. They were reasons I was not old enough to understand.

Although my father had not spoken a complete sentence since the stroke, he and I had our own form of communication. Others talked to him as if there was no intelligence behind the glazed eyes and the vacant expression on his face. They tended to shout as if they thought only a loud voice necessary. If I spoke at all, I spoke quietly. His eyes responded, or more specifically, his good eye responded. Usually I did not have to say anything. When he looked at me I knew what he wanted. His requests were simple. He wanted food or drink. He needed to urinate or defecate. He was too hot or too cold. And most often, he wanted to smoke. When his eyes were open but he was not looking at me, he wanted nothing. When his eyes were closed, he was usually sleeping. But increasingly I was becoming aware of this new message coming from his closed eyes. I knew it meant he wanted me to leave.

I looked back at the basket of green beans. I knew I did not have long. My parents' bedroom had its own door to the outside. It opened onto the yard on the east side of the house. From there I slipped around the corner of the bedroom and I was safely hidden behind the house. It was already hot in the sunshine and the air was hazy with heat. I looked out over the fields. Someone was driving down the lane to the Canton house. A cyclone of dust rose above the hedgerow. I was sure it was my brother. He didn't have a license but Canton let him drive his old pickup on the farm and sometimes even on the highway.

Outside there was only a faint odor of skunk. As I approached the garage I noticed that the padlock was not hooked in the hasp the way we always left it to keep the door from blowing open. The door was slightly ajar and the lock lay on the ground. I wondered if my brother had come out earlier. Perhaps he had intentionally left the door open so the skunk could escape. But why was the lock on the ground? Had he been frightened by a sudden appearance of the skunk, its tail curled back aiming a blast at him?

I found a long stick and, standing to the side of the door, I used it to gently push the door open. I stared into the dark interior for a long time but I could only see the thin lines of sunlight falling through the cracks. Finally I stepped quietly inside and stood very still letting my eyes adjust to the darkness. Inside the odor was very strong and my empty stomach began to churn.

I could make out the litter of car parts on benches and shelves, hanging from nails on the walls. On the oil-caked floor lay a pair of pliers and a ball peen hammer just the way my father had left them. I moved cautiously toward the basket. I could see several jar tops with rotting food in them and one that was dry. Maybe the skunk had died of thirst. I looked back at the door. Perhaps the skunk had escaped. After all someone had left the door ajar. Perhaps it was back in the woods with its own kind, happy and free.

But something was moving through the strips of sunlight. It was Lash Larue. "Lash," I whispered as the skunk came out from behind a radiator. The time was slipping away. My mother might come back to the bedroom at any moment.

Catching the skunk was no problem. It never resisted being touched or petted though it never returned the affection. But picking it up and carrying it out into the bright sunlight was risky. The shock of the sunlight and the fear it might feel being taken from its home could trigger a spray.

I knelt beside it. Its gaze never left me. It seemed to sense that something bad was going to happen. As I curled my fingers under its belly and picked it up, it stiffened, and its tail curled slightly. I tried to point it away from me but it twisted itself with a surprising strength so that my face became the target.

I hurried toward the door and without thinking I passed directly beneath the chain hoist. Something touched my hair, then dropped down on me and slid across my neck and shoulder, its body slick and cool as silk. I seemed to leave my body for a moment and be lifted up into the dark purgatory above myself. From there I looked down and saw myself frozen beneath the dangling ends of the chains, my hands gripping the animal I held too tightly, its body tensed again, its tail curled like a clock spring. And I felt a rope of ice scalding my cheek, my nose, my chest — the dark shiny coil dangling from the hook on the lift chain.

My father's taste in clothes was practical. As a storekeeper he wore sturdy cotton shirts and pants. My mother washed and starched and ironed them. Sharp creases gave shape to the sleeves and pants legs. For church, weddings and funerals he owned two suits. One was called the "new suit" to distinguish it from the other which I presume was older. His church shirts, if he had more than one, were all white. His shoes were black. His only extravagance was a red and black silk necktie, *Made in France*. How he came to possess this exotic article of clothing, I do not know. I have a vague memory of him wearing it to a Christmas party in Lynchburg hosted by the wholesale company that supplied most of the stock for the store. The tie was a statement in color. A bold statement, what I would call today romantic. With his dark hair combed back and his dark skin and eyes, he looked Mediterranean, like a movie star or a gangster. Sometimes in my memory I see a little twist of a smile forming on his lips.

Had it been a snake hanging down from the hook of the hoist brushing my cheek with its cold skin, I might remember it with a laugh as just another time I was frightened as a child. After all, I had always suspected snakes to be hanging from the tier poles. But it was not a snake. It was my father's necktie.

It is impossible for me to say how much I understood then, to separate that knowing from what I have learned and come to believe over the years. I can only tell you what I recall doing after I discovered my father's necktie fashioned into a hangman's noose dangling from the hook of the chain hoist.

I maintained my hold on the skunk, and though its tail remained cocked, it did not spray me. I took it outside and released it into the dry streambed that was the back border of our land. When I put it down, it sat there without moving, looking up at me with pleading eyes. I turned and ran from it, ran back to the garage where I untied the silk tie from the hook and slipped the noose loop through its knot and the silk released its wrinkles and became a necktie again. I folded it and put it in my pocket.

I did not linger. I knew the skunk would try to find its way back into the garage again. It was the only home it knew. I stepped out into the sunlight again and pulled the door closed behind me and fixed the latch. I bent down and picked up the old padlock and hooked it in the hasp. With both hands I squeezed the lock shut until I heard the locking pin snap into place.

I went back to my father's room. My mother was still busy in the store. My father was pretending to sleep but I could sense he knew I was there. I did not hesitate for fear I would lose my nerve. I gripped the sheet and the bedspread that were covering him and peeled them back all the way to the foot of the bed. The odor trapped beneath them rose like fumes from hell. His lids popped open and his good eye skewered me.

His bedclothes and his bedding had to be changed frequently due to his "accidents," as my mother called them. She had become expert at changing the bed with him in it. With my help she would move him to one side of the bed, then unmake the other side and remake it with clean sheets. She would undress and wash him, redress him and with my help move him to the clean side. When the job was completed, we would move him back to the center and she would tuck the sheets in. She could do all this quickly and neatly. I could not. But the bed had to be stripped, my father had to be stripped. I had already decided my mother should never know what had happened.

My father was a small man. Lying there on the white sheet, his left side shriveled from the stroke, he seemed even smaller. I wondered if I could pick him up. In a few years I would grow to be a much bigger man than my father, but on that August morning I had only a child's strength.

I reached down to push him toward the side of the bed. I avoided looking into his eyes, fearing what I might see there. As my hands touched his side, his right hand came up and stopped me. I looked up. The defiance was gone now and what I saw was a look of resignation, something I had never seen in my father before. It only lasted a moment and then he mumbled a word.

"Wait!"

He raised his right leg and swung it to the side of the bed. Then, hooking his knee over the edge he pulled himself across the bed. He reached back with his right hand and grasping the headboard began pulling himself into a sitting position. I stared at him in amazement. I won't say that it was easy. It was not. It was a struggle — but a practiced struggle — and in the end he was standing on his own with his hand against the wall for balance.

I stripped the covers from the bed, balled them into a tight ball, and put them by the outside door. I left the rubber sheet in place covering the mattress and remade the bed with clean sheets. I could not look at my father and in my mind he became someone else — someone I didn't know but was bound to help in this unfortunate situation. He was struggling without success to get out of his pajamas. The smell was strongest on his legs. I unbuttoned his pajama top. Unlike his face and arms, the skin on his chest and stomach was white. The curly black hair lay like a tangle of fish hooks on his chest. I offered my hand to steady him as I shucked the sleeve over his right arm down to the hand that was holding the wall, but he ignored it.

By force of will he took his hand from the wall, teetered a bit, then balanced himself on his right leg while I slipped the sleeve over his hand. The hand then moved quickly back to the wall. I bent down holding my breath against the smell and worked the pajama bottoms down his legs. He lifted one foot. I slipped the pajamas under it. Then, very slowly his other foot arched just enough for me to pull the garment free. When he was completely naked I did not look at him — only parts of him — his feet, his knees — his withered hand hanging by his white thigh. I got soap and water in a pan and washed his knees and legs. By now the smell had dissipated and hung in the room like a smell of mold or wet wool. I dried him with a towel and rubbed his legs with alcohol. I even got some of my mother's hand lotion that smelled like roses and put it on him.

As I drew my hand away from his knee a drop of water splattered on my knuckles and I heard him heave for breath. When I looked up I saw the quivering chin, the wet nostrils, the
steady ribbon of tears sliding down to the point of his chin, collecting, quivering, then falling.

It all turned out quite well. I got my father back to bed and took the clothing outside, hid it and later washed it until the smell was gone. A few days later I found the skunk dead in the highway. There was no odor, just a small mat of black and white fur flattened against the pavement. My father lived another six years. He even learned to walk and to talk again after a fashion. And by the following summer I was free to work in the fields, but I did it only to earn a little money. I knew by then it would not make me a man. That even if it would, I did not want to be one. I kept my father's necktie for many years — first, hidden in my secret place in the wall of my closet along with other treasures; a broken arrowhead I'd found, a pinup of Ava Gardner, an Indian head penny, and the first love letters I ever received. In high school I dreamed of being invited to a sophisticated party somewhere, in some exotic place, where I would appear wearing my father's necktie and be admired and envied by all in attendance. Such a party was never given, or if it was, I was not invited.

Later, when I left home, I carried these things with me locked in a small wooden box. I was in the Army. I worked. I went to school. In 1968 in the City where I was living in a loft with a dozen other people, I knew the party had begun at last. I took the tie from my treasure box and put it on with my faded work shirt and jeans. I tied it first with a simple knot. I was pleased when I looked in the mirror. The tie was unique, just as I remembered it. But something was not right. I loosened the knot and tried to affect a more casual look. This was 1968. Casual? Formal? Those terms were obsolete. Your style had to be far out, outrageous. I looked at myself again and again and finally it came to me. I removed the tie and fashioned it into a hangman's noose, slipped it over my head so that the knot stood up behind my left ear. The wide field of sensuous colors stuck out of the knot like a tongue and curled behind me. Everyone loved it. I walked the streets to rave reviews. Friends and strangers wanted to "hang" with me. For a brief moment I was The Man. But quickly my fame faded. I continued wearing the tie — it seemed to become a part of me — but I gave up the noose.

That could have been the end of the story, but then I fell in love. The tie's importance in my life faded. I still wore it from time to time but it was just another rag, a part of my wardrobe of rags.

It was a fine spring day in 1970 when my love and I bought a kite at a shop on Christopher Street. We walked to the park and assembled its parts. It was a great dragon affair, a kite to brag on, to explore the clouds, but when we let it go in the breeze it bucked and twisted like a wild stallion. Several times we nearly lost it as it spiraled downward out of our control, but at the last instant it swooped up again, just inches from the waves. Finally we coaxed it within reach and brought it down. I knew what was needed. My brother and I had flown kites together all the years of our childhood. It needed a tail.

The silk slipped easily from the collar of my shirt and there I was tying my father's necktie to the tail of our kite. This time the dragon not only twisted and bucked and spiraled, it ascended into the heavens, with a head of steam so great the spinning spool burned my fingers. Three clouds like puffs from a steam whistle dotted the sky. As it passed in front of one of them I got a last look at the long bright tail of the dragon. I did not know how much cord we had on the spool. I let it run on and on until the tension on the line snapped and I was left with an empty spool.

Gaylord Brewer

THE SEA'S ARGUMENT AND AFTER

If I swore to you that the first night,
then each subsequent, the sea crashed
her gavel onto stones diminished
to a verdict of sand, that the first night
and each subsequent she entreated me
and me alone, so finally I opened the flap
of a trembling cabin and, dressed only in shorts,
descended the muddy slope of edges
and darkness to answer her, if I swore this
on my remaining life you would
smile and shake your head, recalling
how I am, believing me a little crazy only if
I really meant it. Go ahead. I meant it.
One couldn't sleep, anyway, hovering on a cot,
supplicant in lightless time and space.
Her cooing roar, her ceaseless thunder,
upheavals that, to a man suddenly
awake and upright in the dark, sounded
his sure, sudden end, the whole stupid hill
and its human wanderer washed away
and why not, now and here? So I went.
The black horizonless sky, the foaming white
of her argument. Enough was enough.
I screamed into the *sturm und drang* that I'd
heard it all before, the bullying options,
each battering old truth, I knew it all already.
Tell me something new, bitch, that I can use.
Okay, maybe now you're a bit worried?
me half-naked and half-baked, you're guessing
a little drunk on cheap rum, two-fisted
and threatening the cold, wild Pacific?
Okay, worry. But if it wasn't me she addressed,
then whom? I was the one there, the one
who showed up, I and a single frantic
bat. As the jungle's night eyes watched,

she embraced me to the waist, towed me
to my knees then onto my back in a tangle
of arms and pain and curses. I slapped my way
back to my feet, stumbled out of reach.
Stood breathing heavily her salt, my blood,
as she hushed and purred, wailed and raged.

Maj Ragain

UP THE STAIRS I RISE TO WAKE THE MOON: EULOGY, DANIEL THOMPSON'S FUNERAL, CHURCH OF THE COVENANT, CLEVELAND, OHIO, MAY 10, 2004

Daniel was, for years, a puckish and welcome intruder in our house in Kent, a first story man. My wife LuAnn would sometimes look up from her reading or work at hand and say, I think Daniel is coming to visit. He would barge through the door unannounced, unbidden, like one of D.H. Lawrence's strange angels. Admit them, admit them, urges Lawrence in his poem. Admit him, we did, gladly. I never got past the bright map of his face, though I do recall he always stomped into the house, a bow legged twostep. His face, an impish grin as if he had let the air out of one of my tires or picked all of the preacher's tulips or committed a misdemeanor for love or justice or both. He arrived hungry. He couldn't eat everything because of his diabetes, but he ate all of everything else, with lip smacking, polishing the plate with bread gusto. Then, the stories would start. Half the people Lu and I didn't know in his Damon Runyon/Mickey Spillane/ Dostoevski/ Cleveland intrigue epics. We listened, not for the facts or the cavalcade of pilgrims in progress, but for whatever it was that moved Daniel, made him rise up in delight, whatever was behind those words like a bee swarm round his head.

In the poetry of Virgil, we find the phrase *lacrimae rerum*, the tears of things, an old and abiding pity, what brokenness knows deep in the chest. Daniel always understood that there are tears inside everything, even words. Especially words. Daniel knew that words are also full of honey. Honey and tears are the marrow of words. Daniel, the poet of tears. Daniel, the poet of honey. Daniel, the poet of vinegar and salt. Daniel, big whiskered wooly hummingbird, found ways everyday to drink from the moment's source, the orange trumpet vine, the blue morning glory, the sweet pea blossom, the rose with petals of concrete, the rusted sunflower.

The first night after Daniel stepped into the shadows, Lu and I lit candles, in mason jars, and set them out on the front steps. I couldn't shake the thought of Daniel flying overhead, circling the earth, unfettered, tumbling like an otter, paddling along on his back, cracking oyster shells with a rock, eating the poems he found inside, pitching the shells down to earth—check your backyard—playing in the Aurora Borealis surf, doing loop-de-loops through the magnetic static of the Van Allen belt, a swimmer in the waning moonlight. Sustained, safe, in the long orbit which cradled him. These candles are navigation lights, little lamps of grief, votive flames of gratitude, little bonfires of love and friendship, landing lights on the deck of the mothership, Krishna's chicory eyes, a constellation in the sky beneath our feet, little tongues of fire making words in the darkness. Light a candle tonight before you sleep your own little death. Set it out under the open sky for the freedom train flyer. Guide him home. All things are an exchange of fire: fire to fire; naked heart to naked heart.

The body is a temporary home. There are only things continually arising and passing away, as is their nature. Everything is preparing to disappear. If you understand this, your heart will ease. Love hard. Pay attention. Be grateful.

As Daniel lay in the hospital bed, Cleveland Clinic, Wednesday afternoon, May 5, Cinco de Mayo, the day before he left, I held his hand and watched his labored breathing beneath the oxygen mask for a couple of hours, the rise and fall of his chest. The abode of his loving heart. Where is breath before we breathe it? If we understand that, we are home. Daniel is going home. In his poems, he mapped the way, blue highways, asphalt, gravel, dirt lowways, a footpath. From there on, it is unmarked. We walk shoeless in the dark. Our homesickness is our guide. Trust that. If you were homeless, you'd be home right now, right here.

Daniel has gone away. No one knows where away is. It may not be far. Away may be no more than the space between two breaths, two heartbeats, or two words, like food, love, home, sing.

Farewell to the poet who kept the watch with the saints in the city and weathered the midnight air.

Farewell to the poet who played the flute cut from articulate bone, music that flowed like a stream of light.

Farewell to the poetry fool who did persist in his folly till he became wise. Few have gone as far down that unmarked trail as Daniel did, hauling the dark cargo of the heart.

Farewell to the poet who wrote his valentine in the ghost snow, who knew that anguish is still the world's official language.

Farewell to the beekeeper stung by death, to the poet who made honey of old failures and regrets. Each poem is a jar of that honey. Each taste carries a blessing, even if hidden. O taste and see.

Farewell to the poet whose question has gone unanswered: O America, cold machine in high fever/Why must you devour the young!

Farewell to the poet who knew, even when lost, there are small dark eyes loving him in secret.

Farewell to the poet who slept under the map of the world and kept time by the heart worn on his sleeve.

Farewell to the poet who shouldered the burden of love's loneliness and taught himself how to live, mouth to hand, hand to mouth.

Farewell to the poet who taught us again and again that the most sublime act is to set another before you.

Farewell to the poet who had the picture of Jesus in his face, who stood like a tree by the water and would not be moved.

Farewell to the poet who sang to the lone sparrow caught in the thicket.

Farewell to the poet who knew we all share one loneliness and one need to break bread and out of that broken silence tumbles everything.

Farewell to the poet who was singular in his disturbance, whose dreams cut like a knife.

Farewell to the poet who was one with the dumb and stood up for the stupid and the crazy.

Farewell to the poet whose cock and bully days are done yet his heart, still shining, sings.

Farewell to the poet who left a trail of breadcrumb words for the alphabet birds that follow us all.

Farewell to the poet who knew we all save coupons no one will redeem except in darkness. Sorrow. Sorrow. Sorrow.

Farewell to the poet who drank the bitter dregs of Winesburg in the dark laughter of rain.

Farewell to the nocturnal poet who stepped through the crack, before dawn, Thursday morning, May 6, not into the heartless dark but into that cornucopia of light for which he yearned.

Farewell to the poet who this day comes to ground zero, upon the down of earth to rest.

Farewell to the poet who waited sixty nine years for the weather to break. This day the weather has broken like a river in our hearts.

> O listen to the silence and the words
> And the silence and the words and the silence
> And the words and the silence…and the words
> And the silence.

Fare thee well and safe passage to Daniel whose name we call out into the honeyed air of eternity. Daniel. Now, quiet as a star.

Cheryl Diane Kidder
LOOK AWAY

He was already dead by the time I saw him. I had to believe that. Although I did see his eyes move, maybe that was a reflex, his eyelashes closing or opening one last time.

By the time I saw him he was propped up in the cage, sitting with his back up against the bars, one arm thrown through them, dangling outside, the massive, impossible head of the lion held momentarily away from his limp body by a second man, a friend, a zoo employee, I couldn't know, who had somehow reached through the bars from outside and grabbed the mane. Who he was or where he came from was never explained to me. But he was leaning away from the beast with all his weight, up on his heels, his hand buried in the mane, his face turned out toward the camera, terrible panic, screaming in a language I did not recognize and yet I could understand every word, as if he was pleading directly to me for help.

This man outside the cage wears red and purple robes and a type of headdress I associate with being from India, or maybe Pakistan. The cage, what I can see of it, this was all shot very close up, is very small, no more than five feet from the bars to the back wall where I can see the back half of another lion laying on its haunches, seemingly unperturbed by the commotion going on inches away.

But, noticing this second lion I hold the knowledge behind me, push it back. If the second lion turned to aid the first, surely there would be no chance at all.

Of course, I always believed the man sitting immobile just inside the cage (how did he get there, was he a caretaker or an employee of the zoo, or had he foolishly and wantonly stepped inside the cage of his own volition, daring fate, the beasts, and nature itself to show him a different outcome, a surprising victory over the beasts, did he hope to somehow step in and step out again, whole, breathing, limbs intact, maybe he knew the lions had already eaten and was hedging his bets that way, or maybe his friend in the red and purple robes had dared him to enter the cage, maybe they had bet on how long he could stand inside the door and escape unharmed, maybe they had been drinking, judgement impaired and the fellow in the white robe, the one now immobile, had laughed and believed it was easy money, maybe he wagered the cost of one more beer, or a round of drinks, to stand inside the bars for one minute, or two, could he last three minutes, maybe his friend in the red and purple robes bet him a day's wages and he could not pass that up, he had to take the chance, maybe he'd seen it done before and as the two friends watched the lions from outside the cage, maybe they appeared old, slow and sleepy, maybe there was a very good chance he could enter the cage, stand silently for three minutes and the two lions would never wake up, never notice at all, maybe he had children or a new wife with a child on the way and the prospect of a day's wages for three minutes of bravery seemed a good bet to take), but he must be gone already, before the video begins. I was sure I would not be watching the actual moment, the last breath, the last tug at the bars, the last blink. I would not be watching that. That would not be filmed, no one would pick up a recorder and stand passively three feet away from this and do nothing but hold the camera steady.

And then, just then, our fellow in the red and purple robes loses his grip on the lion's mane and falls back on the cement floor. In an instant the lion repositions itself in order to close its jaws around the sitting man's neck and our man in the white robes leans a little to the left and you see that the man is still alive because his left arm reaches out to grab onto the bars of the cage, reaches for his friend, reaches maybe an inch off the cement floor, but reaches and moves and there is life there, you can see it, it's unmistakable. But all you can really see of the man is the back of his head and his back, down to his waist, leaning impossibly close against the bars, the rest of his body obscured by the massive bulk of the lion which is now lying completely on top of our man in the white robes, his dark curly hair pushed out between the bars in odd angles.

And you think it might have been that our man walked into the small, cramped cage exactly for this purpose. Perhaps he had dreamed of lions all his life, had seen an attack in his village as a boy and the sight of the mangled body had never left him. Perhaps he became obsessed with lions and violence, attempting to replicate the exhilaration he felt in the dream, in real life, but was never quite able to get to that heart stopping moment he recalled when he finally pushed through the crowd of onlookers to see the piles of blood and bone that had been a man an hour, twenty minutes, three minutes earlier, still steaming in the morning heat, blood like party favors, sprayed onto the autumn corn stalks, now dry and brittle, their once upright bodies now flattened with the weight of what had happened there, and everyone in the village, everyone he knew, standing in a circle, the stalks cracking with the milling of the crowd and the smell, the rotten, fresh smell of the blood and all that was left.

Maybe his parents were long dead and his sweetheart had gone with another man and was having babies that weren't his. Maybe the best thing he could imagine would be to pick up the heavy iron key, carry it to the rusty cage door, slide it into the lock, turn it two full revolutions, listen to the liberating sound of the lock unlatching, the rust falling away, his future and his dream becoming manifest. Maybe he'd opened the door slowly, removed the key, reclosed the door and locked it once again from the inside. Perhaps it was the sound of the tumblers falling into place that had perked up the lion's ear or maybe it was just the smell of the man, so close that turned the lion's head. Perhaps there had been no sound at all.

By the time the video starts there is only the sound of the fellow in the red and purple robes screaming in a language you have never heard, but you understand perfectly what he is saying and the look in his eyes as he pulls with his entire body, his hands somewhere buried in the lion's face or mane. You understand.

What is not immediately clear is whether the man sitting silently with his back up against the bars, the man in the white robes, his back to the camera, is alive and perhaps choosing to remain stationary hoping not to be thought of as prey, or whether he is already dead.

And in the moments while this is still unclear, you make a deal with yourself and the deal is, if the man in the white robes is already dead then this is not so bad. It's not so bad that someone with a camera started filming and it's not so bad that you clicked on the link "Lion Attack," this link, out of all the other possible links, such as "Lion Kills Man," or "Lion Attacks Man in Africa, full video," or "Lion Attacks People," or "Lion Attacks Man and kills him," or "Lion Attacks Hunter in Africa."

It's not so bad because you picked the title that had the least possibility of showing something real, this up close, this clearly filmed, with a soundtrack of this intensity.

And it's just at that moment when you've decided he is already dead that the man in the red and purple robes loses his grip and the lion clamps his jaws around the man's neck and then a third man enters the frame with a long pole and starts jabbing the lion through the bars with the pole that doesn't appear to have a sharpened end, but a round, dull end and this new man gets in five or six jabs before the lion completely repositions itself at the man's feet, clamps his jaws around the man's ankles and leans back with all its weight, back onto its haunches and takes one step back, deeper into the cage, away from the bars, and then he takes another step and another in quick succession, and you realize that the man in the white robes is moving further and further away from his rescuers and you realize the man, all along, was still just a little bit alive because his left arm stretches out back toward the bars for a moment, just a moment and you see willful, purposeful body movement and even though you had just decided this man was already dead, it's clear, too clear, that the man in the white robes was still alive through everything you've been watching and now the man in the red and purple robes and the man with the pole are screaming, but not in a hopeful way, and the lion is leaning all the way back on its haunches and step by step is dragging the man in the white robes away from the bars, further and further until even the man's left arm and hand and the tips of his fingers are out of his rescuers reach and just at that moment, when you see and the lion sees that he has been successful, he loosens his grip on the man's ankles and moves his body, his entire body on top of and over the man in the white robes, leans his massive head back and opens his jaws wider than you thought possible.

And because you're pretty sure that what happens next is going to be even worse than what you have just seen, you click pause and then close the window and you know you need to fill up your eyes with other images as quickly as possible, and you do.

You scan the entertainment news out of Hollywood. You watch a movie. You get out of the house and watch another movie in a theater with a crowd of people around you.

And that night your dreams are full of lions, sitting calmly in the distance, outside their cages, along the path you are on and every way you turn to take a different path there are lions, sitting calmly, gazing out into the distance, waiting.

Shaun Griffin

THESE ARE OLD WINDOWS

I.

They have seen stars
and men hobbled to stones
below their feet, bent
to the truck-bed with bricks
and mortar for the walls
that rise to glass shards

These windows with wood frames
watch the moon give
itself to lovers
with a cigarette
afloat in the smoke
of the Albayzín.

These windows have marched
to the graves of poets, stood erect
with morning glories and
wisteria on the panes,
a thin relief of history
outside the house.

These windows have closed
two centuries of dust and cold
and lies to frame the sun,
a cloud, and dying moon
like Borges, whose eyes
were serpents.

II.

These windows salute
with reflection,
they have no paint
beneath the surface.

They cannot hide from the banal.
They retrieve the day as it falls.

In the morning paper, an Iraqi woman
tears at her dress, her breasts
blind with grief at the loss of her son
in the bed of a truck for stones
that could have been here:
this street, this son, this stone.

And the sons will read other stories
in the window when they rise
to salute the chosen,
and the stones fall
to the patio of orange brick
and a church, and a window.

And whether Christ or Allah
in the glass, the shard of belief
guides the moon to shore in the east,
and the sons to home in the west,
and the brief hours of a flower
open the wooden cheekbones again.

Shaun Griffin

SLEEPING ON THE TERRAZA WITHOUT YOU

For five nights you have risen beneath the canvas
roof and walked the tile fragments—your toes

on the miniature paintings
and once, you were a blackbird

in the grape trellis, spitting the blood
seeds down into the white fan of daybreak,

each turn of sun almost insignificant
where sun has eaten from our lives

for two summers, and the honeysuckle
swallows the ribs of the guardrail without you—

woman who wears white and yellow
like a vine and cannot imagine this morning

without a crawl up the fence of home, miles and
miles to the west where blackbirds discovered land

and brought grapes to the rooftop
of two who cannot for long divide flesh

and become its tutor: the night has breached
and we do not believe the aberration

of one apart from this place you last rested
in the smoke and wind of every breath.

Shaun Griffin

THE LABYRINTH OF THE MIND

for Carolyn Kizer

Now you are truly in the hands of the dispossessed,
nursed into numbness   by women half your age, nursed

into the holy land you wrote of your late friend, Hayden.

This subterfuge, this dying of a mind, is not holy
and it does not want to be such. Your eyes

turn to what they need in this room: the poems
read over and over. And you descend their depths.

I had few teachers. One was you—on that couch

in Mountain View, reading word by word the first book,
written in the catacombs of grad school. Do we ever finish,

this thirty-year interlude with you in the eucalyptus grove
and I on my stone perch in the mountains, do we ever

arc the silence of a mind? You have no strength

to dredge the life-blows and yet this day returns
to the subtle relief of hours together, the diapason

of poetry remembered. This is our truth,
our refuge, our shared, spoken gravity.

Sharon Solwitz

SEX AND DEATH DUKE IT OUT

"We should talk about it," said Allan's wife, *it* being the web of thought and feeling that thwarted their lovemaking.

It was not new territory. New only was her urgency, her dispassionate directness. They were in bed where, Allan had read or heard, you weren't supposed to discuss problems with sex. He touched her face, ran a thumb across her lips. She quivered, her desire palpable and sad. Like the fossil of a beautiful extinct animal.

"Do you remember what it was like to kiss me?" she said.

He did in fact remember. Lips and tongue and beating heart, the feeling of uncontrolled ascent or descent. The continual charged longing, with the desire for both perpetuation and the explosive end. The true oxymoron of feeling.

"Same lips," she said. "Do you think the Angel of Death will come down? If we relax our vigilance?"

There were many wrong ways to respond. He had to push through the reasoning and explaining that gathered in his mind like soldiers with bayonets, to wit: the phalanx of fast-dividing cells in their elder son that might have outwitted the chemotherapy, scouting Nate's blood stream (as Allan pictured it), his lymphatic system, the blood richness of lungs and liver for a new place to camp. So far, Allan could manage his fearfulness with a poultice of pulverized roots that Nate wore to bed for an hour each night. Illusory; Allan was cognizant enough to know that. But it worked, even the illusion of control. Fifteen minutes and he'd go into Nate's room and remove the towel.

"Thea," he said, "you're a remarkable woman."

Should he have said beautiful? She was. But they seemed to occupy a room that, capacious at first, was continually shrinking.

She said, brusquely, "Should we ask The Queen to come up and join us?"

The Queen was the adolescent girl asleep in their basement. Last year she'd have bewitched him—young, pretty, lost in the storm. No boots but a fur coat. A creature out of Dickens or a fairy tale. Out of the dark, the cold, she had found his parked car. Freaky, his first glimpse of her, curled on the seat in back like a furred animal. But she was shivering; how could he eject her? And it was so late, past 10 PM; where else could he take her? "You were great with her," he said to Thea. "You looked like we do it every day, succoring the homeless."

"Did I have a choice? But that coat of hers. Where's *my* silver fox?" The sarcasm might have turned mean but for her ability to change moods on a dime. She slipped a hand under the loose T shirt he wore to bed like a college student, though those years were long gone. He lay still, trying not to watch the clock. "Well," she said, "it's a few Reward Points from the Almighty. And she adds something to the atmosphere, right? Trashy and sweet?"

He sniffed the air, though he knew she didn't mean it literally. Still he could recall the girl's scent when she got in the car, of coconut, it seemed to him, though he might have imagined it. Thea's hand moved along his bare hip. The smell of her shampoo was pleasant, and he touched a curl of her hair, silky and springy like her soul in his opinion, heard her intake of breath. She was so turned on he wanted to weep. He stretched a leg self-consciously.

"Feel free to think about your pretty jail bait," she said. "Go on, fantasize, you have my permission." Her hand continued its travels for better or worse.

"I love you like crazy, Thea."

"Prove it."

He wanted to laugh then, but his throat was too stiff. *If Nate were well,* he thought but didn't say, knowing her response: Either, *he is well,* or *Have some* faith, both painfully wishful. Allan yawned instead, and turned away to conceal it. And Thea, sweet, amused, adorable, was easy on him.

"That coat is real. Do you think she's a hooker?"

"God, I hope not."

"She's stunningly beautiful. I'll try to think of her as the daughter we never had. Do you think that's her real name?"

"Who knows? Why would she lie?"

"Why indeed?" she breathed, weaseling under him, till his body couldn't help but feel hers no matter what his mind had in mind.

Marie Antonett woke on the strangers' sofa bed with the impulse to rob the place. There was wealth upstairs, she'd seen out of the corner of her eye—in china cabinets, in the accounts represented by credit cards to be found in purses and wallets. That she had been trusted, offered shelter on a snowy night—she didn't feel good about it. But it wouldn't be the first time she took things that weren't hers, nor was the sum of her thievery equal in any way to what had been taken from her in her sixteen years: faith, trust, the capacity to love unreflectingly. In the Feinsteins' "rec" room, in a flannel nightgown of Mrs. Feinstein's, she waited for her eyes to adjust to the dark.

But the darkness was so uniform, so apparently dense it seemed a substance, soft and thick like the snow that might still be coming down. *You* try sleeping in vampire land, she said to a face in her mind, of a brainless white girl whose mother lectured her and wept when she missed curfew. This was whom she addressed when there was no one to talk to who might actually respond (and, no, she did not move her lips like a bag lady). She aimed her eyes at where her hands should be but saw nothing, not even when she brought her fingers close enough to her face to feel their heat. Her heart pounded, not with fear—she did not admit to fear—but with an upsurge of clear-headed readiness. Her name was chosen by someone with imperial hopes for her. She had been raped; she had seen dead bodies—two, in fact, and not all laid out in their coffins. She could meet what was coming with what was required.

She got up from the thin foam mattress and set forth, arms outstretched, across the sticky linoleum floor—sticky and icy at the same time (was that physically possible?) She wanted her coat but couldn't remember where she had put it. Seeking walls, a light switch, she picked up each foot and planted it against her squeamishness, pushing through darkness like water till there was a small ripping sound: her flannel nightgown had caught on something. When Mrs. Feinstein placed it in her hands she should have declined, but how? *Thanks, do you have something more, uh, youthful?* She detached herself from a corner of what she recognized as a ping pong table, though last night it seemed to have been in a different place. Oh, for boundaries. She walked gingerly, as if she could thus avoid dirtying her feet, like the girl in her mind whom she loved and hated and should have been. Who wouldn't have left home without slippers lined in bunny fur. Not that the girl would have left home at all, except for a sleepover.

She uttered a light, bitter laugh: Wasn't *this* a sleepover?

In his room on the second floor of the Evanston house where he had lived most of his fourteen years, Nathan Feinstein lay in bed in his pajama pants. Shirtless. On his back. Spread across his belly was a kitchen towel, and under it the paste—drying now—that his father had pureed in the Cuisinart (eye of newt, toe of frog, said his mother) to keep him well. The drying paste was starting to itch, and Nate was trying not to move or scratch, but that was the only thing that bothered him. Before he got sick, he had suffered intermittent bouts of terror at the thought of dying. At nine, ten, eleven, every few months his legs would go weak, his heart race at the thought of Not Being, which seemed, then, imminent. To lose the smell of trees, the taste of mint chocolate chip ice cream, how his legs felt running, the pure pleasure of being lifted in someone's arms for an unobstructed view of the world, and all the things he couldn't imagine but knew he would like—he'd lie rigid on the couch in the den with covers over his head till his brother came in to harass him, or Dad, to see what was wrong. And now, with a disease that people were scared to name in his presence, in that anxious, fragile state called remission (in which only 31% with his disease remained for five years), he no longer thought about death, or about anything in his shadowy future. There was just *now*, the itchiness of his dad's herbal paste, to be assuaged when his father came to clean him up (half-hour to go). Careful not to disturb the towel and the salutary herbs beneath, he turned a light on and read a chapter of *Crime and Punishment*, hoping Raskolnikov would change his mind. He could just rob the old woman, he didn't have to kill her. In the chapter, Raskolnikov received a letter from his sister, who was about to marry someone wealthy. There would be money now for him to go back to school, but for some reason Raskolnikov became even more desperate. Was Nate like him in any way? He looked at the clock: The half hour was long gone.

Marie Antonett found the wall of the Feinsteins' rec room (wreck room?), which felt like painted cinderblock. How insulting, that these people with their high-end first floor, all golden wood and tile and thick rugs, had stashed her in their crappy basement. Another reason to relieve them of some of their cash. Moving clockwise she patted her way along the wall, which was disturbingly rough and cold (almost moist!), deeming the Feinstein house a metaphor for rich people's lives, glamour with a rotten underside(!), as her English teacher had described Daisy and Tom's life in *The Great Gatsby* (she did well in school, not that Aunt Teena cared if she even got up for it). Maybe this was the little Feinsteins' punishment place. *Mouth off again and it's the cellar for you. No, I'll be good, Daddy!* Not that a man who cared whether a stranger froze to death in the night seemed the punishing type.

Then the switch appeared under her fingers. There was light; the room shrank and ordered itself. There was her shirt, her Skinny Mama jeans (a good knock-off). But no coat—the one nice thing Aunt Teena owned. Marie Antoinett envisioned tomorrow at the Feinsteins' front door, thanking them for the breakfast they would have served her, being handed an old parka. Mr. Feinstein gallantly helping her into it: *This will keep you plenty warm.* Mrs. Feinstein: *What does a young girl need with fur?* But even tired and nervous as she was, the scenario seemed far-fetched. Mrs. Feinstein might not have warmed to her husband's idea of an overnight guest but she would not have stolen the guest's coat (would she?). They were harmless, like parents from old TV shows who played catch with kids and grounded them when they stayed out late. They would have hung Marie Antonett's coat in a closet with the Feinstein overcoats, over a row of Mrs. Feinstein's leather boots, which, whatever the style, would be a step up from what Marie Antonett had set on their mat. She'd have a choice of footwear, like in a shoe store.

She opened the door to the stairs wondering if Mrs. Feinstein was the type to take her purse into her bedroom or leave it out on a polished tabletop. She did not want to think about Mr. Feinstein. They would have money left over. And a story to tell. That she had given them. It was her thank you.

She wasn't trying to be funny. Well, maybe kind of.

After the small shock of being forgotten, Nate was glad for the lapse, that his father's overweening concern could wander past him. Using both hands to keep the paste-laden towel against his abdomen, he stepped out into the hallway. There was a slight, sharp pain in his back but he ignored it—in the past eight months he had felt much worse. Its locale was new, just below his left shoulder blade, but it was a *one* or *two* on the doctors' pain scale in which *ten* was the worst. And it was somewhat familiar, like the stitch in his side he got sometimes toward the end of a basketball game. As he tried to pinpoint the pain, perhaps to tell his mother about it in the morning (Dad would take it too seriously), it disappeared altogether. Goodbye.

In the bathroom he stood over the toilet bowl and carefully peeled off the towel so that the clots of paste hit the water. He bunched the towel around whatever was left of his father's concoction and stowed it in a corner. There was some on his PJs. These he dropped and, before washing, examined himself in the mirror, considering whether, to a total stranger, the long scar down his belly looked like it came from a knife fight. The pain in his back was completely gone, so it did not (he was almost sure) signal new tumor growth. From what he knew all too well, tumors didn't vanish without help. More frightening was Raskolnikov sewing a loop inside his coat for the murder weapon, an axe. Face down on the nightstand beside Nate's bed, the book was waiting.

For Marie Antonett, opening the door to the kitchen was like rising up to heaven. No lights were on here either—this family was Green!—but the pale oblongs of the windows softened the darkness; the kitchen counter glimmered as if with its own tiny lights. The floor tile was broad and slippery smooth, and clean; not a crumb. She padded on pleasuring soles to the refrigerator, hoping for a diet root beer. There were no diet drinks, though, just an array of small bottles with names like Ambrosia, Carrot-Lemon Grass, Strawberry-Kiwi (100% fruit). She tried Ambrosia, which was nasty; she poured it into the sink. Strawberry-Kiwi was all right. To her surprise, the refrigerator pulled shut as soon as she let go, as if it had its own mind. She tried again, opened the door all the way, and laughed when it tried once more to close itself. No one in this house would get slapped for spoiling the milk! Door open against her hip, she regarded the counter in the soft refrigerator light, the clusters of small shiny appliances, some of which she didn't recognize (Aunt Teena had a toaster oven). She admired the tidy, courteous groupings at the back of the counter, imagining what it was like to live in this house. Mom making everyone finish their crunchy granola? This was a crunchy granola household, she was sure. Granola hurt her back teeth.

By the clock over the stove she saw she didn't have to hurry. There were hours till this family got up. On the other side of the kitchen was a small room with a washer, dryer and tub-size sink, at the far end of which another door opened onto a garage. There were two cars, the second classier than the one she'd been driven in.

She walked back the way she had come—this house was a monster—through the kitchen into the dining room, the living room, and sat down experimentally on the long curving sofa, leather but marshmallow soft. She tried a chair with equal pleasure then stretched out on the rug, spread hands and feet, touched nothing. She loved the room, the fireplace, the bank of windows over the wide lawn. But there was business to accomplish.

Across the room an archway led to the foyer and the front door and a staircase curving upward. Here was a genuine coat closet, packed full. But these were wool coats and parkas; hers was not among them. She glanced up the lushly carpeted stairs, imagining Mrs. Feinstein transporting her coat to a special place with controlled humidity (what was wrong with humidity?). Beside the front door was an umbrella stand painted with a Japanese woman holding a parasol. Ceramic. Breakable. She picked it up, in the mood to break things. But not now; not yet. Checking the Feinstein family coat pockets she found ticket stubs, crumpled facial tissue, a pair of thin leather gloves, a tube of lipstick. The lipstick she palmed though there was no place to stow it, her nightgown having no pockets. The gloves fit and she left them on.

Suddenly she wanted to cry. She sat down on the stairs, put her face in her gloved hands. At the same time a flutter and hum rose up all around her as if the house were clearing its throat. It was only the furnace kicking on but she was trembling. She was cold. She needed her coat. They had her fucking coat. Then she was climbing, quickly, soundlessly, the carpeted stairs. She would not, of course, accuse her hosts in their beds; she would simply tiptoe around till she found what was hers and, if she were lucky, something of theirs too. Gloved fingers leave no prints!

The upstairs looked smaller than the floor below, a hallway with one door to the right, three to the left. From the right hand door came a series of rising moans she couldn't help but recognize. How many kids lived here? The one boy she'd met was too young for sex. Picturing Mr. and Mrs. Feinstein in the act of making these sounds made her step back involuntarily. All she had eaten yesterday, besides nasty beer, was a handful of cheese-flavored Doritos but the back of her throat clenched. A barf was coming, which she could not bear to deliver upon the clean hall carpet. She scurried left around a bend toward what she hoped was a bathroom, opened a half-open door—and had to squelch her shriek. In front of the sink stood a boy with a washrag in his hand, taller than she and butt naked. His genitalia made her think he was sixteen or seventeen but he was slim and his face was smooth and round. She pressed herself against the doorframe. "Oops," he said.

Suddenly she wanted to laugh. "*Oops?* Who the fuck says 'oops'?"

In the light from the hanging globes over the mirror his face reddened, but he made no move to cover himself. His dick was as man-size as any she had seen. "Excuse me," he said. "I thought you were my brother."

"Do I look like your brother?"

He laughed. "But I have to clean up. I'm still kind of itchy."

She stepped back but not so far that he could close the door. Not that he seemed to think it necessary. He was either unaware of her gaze or else unwilling to hurt her feelings by closing her out. For some reason she was inclined toward the latter, not that she knew anyone else who thought like that. He wiped his chest and torso then shook the rag over the toilet; something plinked into the bowl. He rinsed the rag and hung it on the rack, slow like an old person but graceful. Only when he was perfectly clean did he wrap a towel around his waist. "I must look like a freak," he said, with a smile that evinced concern more for her than for himself.

She felt light-headed. His shame, if he felt shame, was on an absurdly small scale. Who was this boy? This dork who didn't see his own dorkiness? She touched his arm. "Want to hook up?" He became utterly still, his wide eyes open on her. She stared back while truth dawned. "Lord God, you don't know what I mean!" She laughed, ramping it up a little. "But, dude, you are hung."

He grabbed a towel from the rack then noticed the one around his waist. His ears, which stuck out a little, were bright red. His hair looked like it would curl if it weren't cut so close to his scalp. He'd look all right if he let it grow. There was a dab of paste on his shoulder. Involuntarily she reached out. "You're wearing gloves," he said.

"Obviously." Embarrassed she peeled them off. She set them side by side on the towel rack, carefully, restoring her dignity.

"I know who you are," he said. "My dad picked you up by Whole Foods."

"So?"

"My mom thinks you're—" He stopped, as if afraid of hurting her feelings.

"She's a bitch," she said.

"She's not!"

She snorted. "Don't get all gallant now."

Some boys, she knew, would have slugged her but this one was easily soothed. He acted like her presence in his house was a gift under the Christmas tree, though she had seen no Christmas tree. This was a boy used to receiving gifts but nonetheless grateful. She felt a pulse of almost genuine warmth. "Let's go down and fuck on one of your folks' pretty rugs. What grade are you in?"

"Eighth."

She let out a hoot then pushed it back. She almost liked him. "You look like you're in high school," she said, though it was only half true.

He excused himself to go to his room for a minute. They exchanged names, as if in parting something might happen and they would need a way to locate each other.

Nate put on fresh pajamas and bedroom slippers, under the spell of her name. Marie Antoinette, queen of France, had been beheaded during the Revolution, bad fortune that had nothing to do with *this* Marie Antoinette, whose life force was so strong he didn't want her out of his sight. He wanted to touch her skin the color of fields in the late afternoon sun, the color gold would have been if it meant anything.

He found her downstairs in the kitchen in front of the refrigerator, from which she had taken a bottle of white wine. She added a jar of capers and an unopened wedge of cheese to the things on the counter. "You got us a good strong rubber?" she said.

Her words at first did not compute. She closed her eyes then opened them again. "A condom. A love glove. What all did you go for?" She raised a finely arched eyebrow. "What do you white boys say? Prophylactic?"

She crisped the consonants. "Sorry," he said, while a world he had only dimly conceived unfurled before his mind's eye. He was on the brink of apologizing again but felt its wrongness. He looked at her, this girl who knew things. She didn't look black, or African American, if that was the right word. She looked, just, *golden.*

"Hey," she said, "do you happen to know where your mom put my coat?"

He shook his head. His sweat glands were gushing. It was like someone had turned a knob inside him.

"Maybe you know where she keeps her purse?"

"No," he breathed.

She looked at him, straight and cool like the woman they called the bad doctor: *You have a tumor in your belly the size of a football.* His sides were wet, and his neck, his hands. "Don't go away," he said. "What's the matter?"

She sighed then tugged at the waistband of his fresh pajama bottoms, white with thin blue stripes. "These have got to go. You look like an old man."

"You're kind of bossy," he said, smiling so that she wouldn't think he was passing judgment.

* * *

They decided to hang out in the basement, for privacy, her idea. The matter of the coat had receded now. She arranged the wine, cheese and capers on the ping pong table, while Nate looked for a corkscrew and paring knife. Capers, she said to herself. The name seemed wrong for the tiny dark green things but right for their briny, sour taste. Bright white light shone on the green-painted table. Taped to the walls were children's crayon drawings. "You did those?" she said to Nate upon his return.

"Not recently," he said, flushing. "Some are Dylan's."

She cut the cheese into thick slices and wolfed them down with a caper or two. She was starving. She could have eaten half a chicken. "This room is ugly," she said, though she didn't mean it. She uncorked the wine. "What are you looking at?" she said to Nate, who looked away apologetically. "I look wack in this nightgown?"

He shook his head.

"Well, you look wack. That shit all over you."

"It's taro root. My father has the idea—"

"Your father's weird."

"No, he's not."

"Chill," she said. "All rich folks are weird."

"We're not rich, we're middle class."

She sent him up again, this time for wine glasses, and while he was gone she took off her gown. When he returned, he didn't seem to notice naked body. He picked the flannel thing off the floor. "That's my mom's," he said, frozen with it in his hands. Again she wanted to laugh.

"You're fourteen and you act like you're nine!"

When he remained stalled out on the linoleum tile in his PJs and slippers, she snatched the gown back and tossed it in a corner. She pulled at the snap on his pants.

It was not a dream. But it felt like dreams he'd had in which he opened a high window of a bedroom like his own and peered out at a spreading landscape that looked like his neighborhood but far down, a long drop. If he could overcome his fear, he would think, he'd be able to fly. And sometimes it worked. He'd climb onto the sill, give his body to the air, and find himself flying like a bird or Superman over the tiny trees and houses, the playground across the street, his pleasure and freedom feeding each other, freedom intensifying pleasure till his chest wanted to explode with swelling joy. Now, sitting cross-legged with Marie

Antonett, both of them naked on the sofa bed, he touched the dark hair that curled down to her breasts, and she seemed not to mind. His hands were happy with their choices. He straightened a curl, let go; it sprang back stubbornly. He touched the smooth cool side of her breast. Sometimes her breath would speed up and she would stop his hand where it was and exhale. His dick throbbed to the point of pain, but he couldn't scale this kind of pain. He shuddered though he wasn't cold.

While he touched her she told him stories. She was the great-great-great granddaughter of Liliuokalani, the Hawaiian queen dethroned by the United States of America. When she got some money together she was going to fly there to reclaim her kingdom. "You don't believe me," she cried, and he swore: Queen of France, Queen of Hawaii, he already believed—his heart racing with fear of hurting her feelings till she went on to the topic of her mother, who, if she wasn't dead, ought to be, for foisting her on Aunt Teena who wasn't even her real aunt and who was definitely *not* getting her coat back (like she could call the police!). Not to mention, that coat being earned by her, over and over again, cleaning the house since Teena wasn't about to, and keeping her sleeves down at school to keep the foster money coming (Teena's nails could rip out your heart in half a second.) *You can stay here with us,* Nate wanted to say but didn't want to stop the flow of her voice. *Who are you?* He was afraid she had dropped down to earth for this one night; tomorrow she would return to her home planet. And what to do with his dick, which seemed to have its own ideas about her.

Then her mood changed. She wandered back to the food and began eating again. He joined her, stuffed his mouth with cheese, capers. They were pigs! Giddy with their shared nakedness, he chased her around the ping pong table and caught her, naked against him. He was fearless of hurting her, neither of them imagining that a touch from one of them could hurt the other, and when they wanted to shriek they pressed their mouths to each other's flesh so as not to wake the house. Were the doors closed? He checked; they they were. Can we lock them? They could not; neither door had a lock or even a hook. They laughed at the lack of security, then at the thought of being seen, of someone actually coming downstairs while they were like *this!* It was crazy mad funny. They screamed with laughter at would-be onlookers.

By now they were casual in their nakedness. They played ping pong, and though Nate wasn't that good a player, in fact lost to Dylan more than he liked to admit, now that he couldn't take his eyes off his partner he couldn't miss, his goal not to win points but to place the ball where she could return it. Do not go to Hawaii, he told her in his mind, though he couldn't imagine after tonight her being anywhere but here. Paddle in hand she walked around in her skin as if it were clothing. She lay down on the fold-out bed and beckoned. She seemed neither clothed nor naked, only herself, this girl who lived inside her golden skin.

To his surprise now, she was interested in his body. His scars—the small fading one by his collarbone, the thick vertical one down his belly. She touched them with fingers whose nails were chewed down to reddish nubs. Under her light, damaged fingertips his scars felt friended, by someone like him who had survived dangers, and he kissed her fingers to restore them, feeling the surge in himself of unfamiliar powers. He was changing as a result of her; becoming, he thought, worthy of her. He wondered if, in a past life, he might have known her. Before *Crime and Punishment* he had read *Siddhartha*. "Do you believe," he said, "in reincarnation?"

She laughed rudely; he tried to explain: That you died and came back in a different form, that you vanished and returned in higher and higher forms until you learned what you were meant to learn—it seemed *fair*. Not that he would mind coming back as a bird or a fish (he loved to swim). If a human being, he hoped to be super tall in his next life, able to dunk in a regulation basket. "It makes more sense," he said, "than heaven and hell."

She snorted. "Who believes in heaven and hell?"

He regarded her, not hopelessly. There was a gap between them; he had to bridge it. "What *do* you believe in?"

"Let's drop this." She raised her chin, eyebrows thickening. She seemed disgusted with him.

"You're the most beautiful girl I've ever seen," he said. "I have to know what you *think*."

For a second he thought she was going to cry. Then her face tightened up. "It's all so much shit."

"Shit?

It was a figure of speech, of course, but the word with its ugly image filled Nate's mind, pushing belly to belly against the idea of reincarnation. He remembered a conversation between his parents in which his mother said, Shit happens, and his father, who could have argued, sat still his chair at the kitchen table while his body seemed to grow smaller. The girl was smiling but not warmly.

"I need a favor," she said. "Do you all keep any money around?" He made no response and she went on. "Like in a drawer? Teena keeps her tips in a cigar box behind the silverware, she doesn't know I know."

"It's in the bank," he said, remembering shortly afterward the stash of twenties in his father's sock drawer. In case of emergency. It had been shown to them in a kind of formal display, even Dylan was there. Not mentioning it to her seemed disloyal. So did telling her. "I really hope," he said desperately, "that if we are reborn, we come back to our same families."

"Touch me," she said.

She lay back on the bed and invited him to touch her anywhere. Some places were better than others. Some she liked enormously. He was painstaking. Some places felt moist and warm to the touch, some almost hot. More, she said, moaning, and he liked making her moan, he liked everything that issued from her. "You have a huge dick," she said.

He nodded gravely. "It might be the treatments."

She laughed and kissed his mouth. "It isn't bad, it's a *good* thing." She didn't ask what treatments.

When she at last touched his dick, he had no doubt it was a good thing. He liked the word dick. Dick. She pulled him toward her and guided him into a place he had heard about but completely failed to imagine.

Afterward, in the dregs of pleasure, he remembered his old fear of death. He wasn't exactly afraid now, but he felt its proximity like a criminal outside a flimsy door; he lay still on the fold-out bed under the white fluorescence. Then she touched him again, and he rose obediently to fill her hand. Beyond, outside, Death fluttered helplessly.

When dawn shone in the basement room's small high windows, Marie Antonett deemed herself stupid. This sort of messing around could get a girl pregnant. She asked Nate for her coat please, and the gloves she'd accidentally left in the bathroom, and money if he could scrounge some, and he was eager to oblige. He came down with everything including a check for $215. "From my grandmother. For my birthday. My age plus one to grow on." It was dated two months ago. "I must not need it since I never cashed it," he said.

It was less than she'd hoped. "You got anything else?" she said.

His look was so full of pain she didn't know what to make of it. There was a silence in which she tried to remember what they were talking about. "I have to ask my dad," he said.

"Forget it. So you're two hundred and fourteen years old?"

"Younger than Methuselah. No, I mean she starts with a base of two hundred." They smiled at each other for different reasons. "When I'm fifteen, I'll get $216."

"I get the picture."

He signed the back of the check, and she spelled her name for him: *Pay to Marie Antonett Collingwood,* and of course he had to start an argument. He enunciated (while she rolled her eyes), "An—*twa*—net. Tee O Eye, right? Like Marie Antoinette, the queen of France."

He was so annoying. "I know, fuck you, she had her head cut off. She said *Let them eat cake* so she maybe deserved it. Do you think I'm so dumb I can't spell my own name?" He wrote it according to her instructions but it rankled. "What would you do," she said sternly, "if you made me pregnant?"

"I would marry you," he said with his wide open smile. "I would marry you if you weren't!"

It was the right answer. Why was she sad? She kissed him and sent him to bed before his parents got up. "See you tomorrow?" he said.

"Maybe." She wrapped herself in her coat, stuffed her new gloves inside an interior pocket and lay back on the bed. "Switch off the light, okay?" The gloves were too thin to keep her hands warm but they were soft and well made; she was glad for them. It was almost tomorrow, one more, perhaps tolerable, day.

Upstairs in his room Nate lay on top of the covers replaying the night from the moment he had seen her outside the bathroom door to the way she had looked wrapped inside the fur of her coat. Like a grown woman, like a cold little girl. Like a giant caterpillar about to molt into full adult beauty. For the third time tonight he took off his pajamas and offered himself to whatever the universe's inscrutable will had in mind.

Julie Marie Wade

PRELUDE (What I Wish Had Happened)

That the sea had risen in sudden fury—
over the bulkheads lacey with moss &
jagged with barnacles & bits of shell;
over the slippery rocks & the dark
trenches of sand pocked by clams
still breathing beneath them; over
even the splintered, lice-ridden logs.
Then, with the vigor of something
like love—over the promenades also
& the footpaths arcing into the woods,
over the ball fields with their broken
fences & the battered Poison Ivy signs.

That the sea had kept rising through
the city park, its horseshoe pit shaded
by lilacs, its swing sets ancient &
loosely hinged. That it had flowed
onto Fauntleroy Way in time with
the evening rush; that the row of cars
waiting for their ferry ride home
were left bobbing there, chrome
buoys in a salt-drenched storm.

That the sea, which I had always known
was coming for me, came at last—
gliding diligently over concrete; scaling
the grassy banks with its liquid fingers;
pouring through the latticework of
the red gate that separated our yard
from all the others; then rising to the
height of the picture windows where I
picture my parents still: together

winding their grandfather clock, slashing
each square on the half-cellophaned
calendar. Which is to say—*sad*, without
knowing they are sad, frightened of
time moving & time standing still.

This sea will fracture that glass, & with it,
the tiny, treacherous globe of all my past
lives, even the old paperweight world
resting on the desk, smoothed with felt on
the underside to keep it from slipping away.
Of this I am certain: what we can't stop, in the
end, we destroy. But if, miraculous & auspicious,
a flood begins, like the hired gun of the heart's truest
intention, we surrender everything—
merchandise & misgivings, the old
grudge & the future plan, until even
the baby grand is newly repurposed,
a boat seeping its soggy music, tender &
futile against the faithless white spume.

Obliteration, we say; *or a new beginning.*

Julie Marie Wade

PERIPETEIA

It's like being eighteen again,
the way you can only listen to
so much soft music in a dimly lit room
before something has to perforate or puncture

the needle stick, or unstick

Your heart a feathered thing,
a quilled, willful thing—*porcupine heart*—
ferocious & abysmal, desperate to pierce
someone else's skin in order to dull its own pain

So you say to the man you don't love yet
 (may never love, though you know you're supposed to...),
 breath thick in the throat of the body you don't love yet
(may never love, aren't even supposed to...)

"Will you go down to the vending machine?
Will you bring back all the chocolate & a cherry Coke, too?"
He says, "Now? Right now?" Sweaty at the nape of his neck &
worried, wanting to please you the way candy would, the way caffeine

is this a test? is this only a test?

 So when he's gone in his stocking feet &
the radiator is burning hot like the coals in your father's
old kamado pot & you are without your buttons & your best sense,
the bobby pins your mother taught you to twist in your hair—*disheveled*,

she might call you now—but remembering a story book
where the princess took bed sheets & tied them together, descended
the trellis fashioned from the remnants of her *coitus interruptus,* into the
     night,
into the more-than-night of the equinox, onto a road half-paved &
     entirely abandoned

129

Are you that woman? Will you be that woman once
or in perpetuity—her ankles shackled to the last outpost of moonlight
on the last path that leads to a lake without a boat ramp—a *Last
    Summer at Bluefish Cove*—
which is where you're headed anyway, whether you know it or not.

a tremor, like someone turned the snow globe over

You hear him knocking. "You locked me out!" he'll say.
But you don't answer. His shoes dangle from the telephone line. A prank,
a small amusement to pass the time. "Let me in! Let me in!" he'll say,
    his voice
growing louder like the Wolf in another story you read, once upon a
    time, before bed.

But you deal in riddles now. Even fables are far too long to recount.
You slip a note, perforated, under the door. That quill heart still good
    for something after all.

Jennifer DeJongh
ILLUMINANT

We sisters—
    Cassie, Florrie, Emily, Tabitha. Justine, Christine, Francine, Yvonne. Rebecca, the sweet one. Trudi, the slut. Emma, who says she doesn't have a drug problem. Maricela (adopted). Cookie and Terri (the twins). Hazel, Beatrice, Marilyn
    —Well. You begin to understand.

We planned a picnic. Starr had the idea, and so she organized the collection of baskets and coolers, the wiping of damp paper towels along the bottoms to pick up the dust bunnies they'd gathered from languishing on the top shelves of our coat closets and in our disused sewing rooms. Tracy Lou designed the invitation, and Carol put herself in charge of procuring all our addresses.
    Betsy and Jenn bought the garbage bags and the extra tongs and the plastic bags for leftovers and many of the other things that they claimed no one paid them back for later. (We paid them back. We're sure of it.) Lacey found her old blue-and-white vinyl tablecloth under her daughter's bed in a bin and sent out the call for others.

The forest is a forest forged from our memories and at its tumbled margins it dissolves into a golden field, its dissolution carrying our tables also into the sea of grasses. Stand at a distance from our picnic and you'll see it as it might look if it was only a painting, created with thick dripping brushes in sloppy, broad slashes. The primary colors of our scavenged cloths are pinned among the trees and in odd folds at the legs of the tables we carried upside-down on the tops of our cars or emerging awkwardly from the backs of our trucks and SUVs. These colors melt and mix in the sunlit meadow. They collect a nameless depth from the damp shade of the trees.
    Dahlia, with her coveted movie star name and her unfortunate hairstyle (and it isn't even the pink streak, really, but something more insidious), stands hypnotized by the light moving through the trees and across the sea of color we have wrought. But then she's the one who brought the pot, gallon Ziplocs of the stuff.

Some of us take a walk before eating.

Some of us, because the others have taken a walk, find ourselves slaving over the hot dogs and the burgers and the soy-based patties. 'What is that?' Louise asks. 'Are we sure this is food, darlings?' 'Fucking Gwen,' says Laurie, 'she thinks we have to make something special for her so poor widdle cows won't have to die for her highness. Fuck her, you know?' (The sentiment is echoed by many of us.) 'Whatever ,' says Bethany with her waves of cherry-colored hair and a tattoo so new that the skin of her forearm seems a reflection of her hair. 'I get where she's coming from.'

'You have to be out of your head,' Doris says. She sips white wine from a plastic cup and grimaces. 'To deliberately scar your body like that. Really. If I still had skin like hers —'

Bertha says: 'Oh, this wine is good.'

And Doris says: 'It's cheap. From a box. There's a spigot.'

'Speaking of cheap,' Nancy says, 'She should've just spent the extra money to get one that looks good. I mean, it's your *body*.' (We'd have said Nancy was in the anti-tat faction.) 'Nan, do you have one?' Paige asks, but Nancy holds up a finger tipped with a glossy champagne-colored nail and looks at us from beneath a sexy flip of her pretty bleached hair. 'Work it out yourselves, bitches,' she says and walks away to root up another can of PBR from one of the hundreds —

Thousands? We stopped counting

—of coolers we've arranged under the trees.

Nicole is the one we envy for her legs. She's got those long bowed legs like a model's. We heard once that you can only be a model if your knees don't touch when you stand with your feet together. Collectively we've spent probably thousands of hours standing in front of mirrors with our feet together trying to arch our knees away from each other.

And Nicole's skin shimmers without lotion or roll-on glitter or droplets of pool water. Without anything. Her skin is covered always with a light sheen of sweat that makes her gleam. Some of us think we hate her. 'She'll come down with shit-tons of acne,' Jaime says. 'I miss acne,' says Barbara, and she puts her hand to her throat where the skin is soft and thin as tissue. Amy, the eyeroller, rolls her eyes. She wears this iridescent navy blue mascara —

They use fish scales, we heard, for the iridescence. One day we'll bust out that little fact and blow Amy's mind

— so no one will miss her epic fucking eye rolls.

We ultimately decide that Barbara hasn't noticed. Since her kid died of that lung infection, she hasn't really noticed much of anything. The realization makes us feel better. But we know it shouldn't.

Rosie who gives a crap about almost none of us says: 'Has anyone heard from Mara lately?'

Mara, the one who wants to save the world. Or something.

Mara would have received her invitation far too late (if she got it at all), finding it pressed into her muddy hand by a young man with a t-shirt on backwards and no shoes and several gaps where teeth might be in another man when she emerged slickly from the wet leaves and incessant noise of whatever forest she was currently submerged in, half-dead from diarrhea and some kind of parasite they will determine later. ('Botfly?' we'll suggest, as *botfly* is the only thing we've heard of, and some of us will shudder in horrible pleasure at the idea that we have a sister with a botfly, but 'No', she'll say. 'Not a botfly. Something nameless. I'm just so fucking tired all the time.'), her backpack emptied of food and full of tiny labeled vials of insects.

But Mara hasn't shown. It's not that she's special either. Lots of us haven't shown. We suppose we know why.

Cora, who went to Mexico. Anna, who was murdered.
Ruth, who saw God.
You can't rush birth, Ruth knew, whatever form it took. A life knew its own clock, and so she didn't speed up, only put her hands which were cold at the fingertips into her coat pockets and set one foot in front of the other silently across the sidewalk towards her fate.

The child looked strange once she had got it home and set it onto the couch. Like a throw pillow you picked up on the spur-of-the-moment. Wrong shade, wrong shape, the fringe not reading as edgily bohemian as you had originally expected.

Ruth didn't know many songs for babies. She hadn't really expected to get one so soon and so hadn't boned up on all the fairy tales and things, and so she sang: "Rock-a-bye, baby, in the treetop. When the wind blows, the cradle will stop." (Which didn't make sense but at least rhymed.) 'When the wind stops, the cradle will burst, and out will come…" But that was as far as she got before the melody and the rhymes drained out of her. "Something about a knife," she said. "And— I don't know."

133

She stroked two fingers across the baby's brow, and its hair was like touching a feather and its skin so soft and bruisable. Ruth kissed the baby at the top of its forehead. "Don't cry," she said. But the baby didn't make a sound—and didn't that mean it was a sure thing that it had been God who had delivered it into Ruth's arms? Ruth was flooded with such joy when she realized this that she pressed her mouth too hard against the baby's hairline and it made a noise under her teeth.

"Oh, don't cry," said Ruth, even though now she knew the baby wouldn't. "I'm your new mama." Just saying the word "mama" made Ruth feel a little light-headed. The word squeezed up into her head and spilled from her eyes. "I'm your new mama," she said hoarsely. "I love you so much." It felt amazing, the crying. Like she was finally baptizing her own child with the salt from her body.

Ruth had seen the first mother leaning into the car, buckling in the baby, wrestling with things. An unlit cigarette dangled from the same fingers that tucked the blanket around the child. "Jesus Christ will you sit still," Ruth heard the woman say, and when she left to go into the house for whatever reason—to get a purse, find a match, gather up a second child and the flotsam of it—she left the car door wide open and the baby just sitting there unwatched. A terrible thing for a mother to do. A dangerously irresponsible thing. A thing breathtaking in its arrogance. The baby could be taken. Could untangle itself from the car seat and fall into the road and be crushed in more ways than one.

Ruth, upon reaching the car, saw that the mother's behavior didn't seem to have affected the baby (emotionally speaking) and took it to mean that things were progressing as they were meant to. She almost collected the blanket too but it smelled of old smoke, and so she left it crumpled in the car seat and the door open as it had been when she approached.

Maybe the mother wouldn't notice anything missing. Maybe God would mist over her eyes, and she'd begin carrying around that blanket, clutching it in a bundle like it still had a baby in it, even believing that it did. People would call her crazy and talk about her while she was in the room like they did with Ruth. Ruth carried the baby around the corner, back to her own house. Trying to walk normally so they would draw no attention.

That's how we assume it happened.

This baby didn't cry. Maybe it didn't yet understand the necessity of it.

Or maybe it understood more than Ruth about the necessity of silence. Silence had so far been critical to their success as a family. If not for silence, her daughter would still be strapped into that grimy car seat while the woman who'd strapped her in ashed cigarettes out the window on the highway and poked at her sightlessly when she fussed.

Ruth named her Silla.

We don't approve of the name. It doesn't sound like a name to us. 'Where the hell did she get it?' Betty says. 'Why not Susan? Or Sandra?' 'Stephanie,' Dana suggests. 'Does it have to be an S-name?' Lucinda asks. 'I always liked Hannah. Or Natalie.' 'How could Ruth do that to a child?' Iris demands. 'I just want to know.'

It's not a name we're comfortable with. It's just a word that Ruth plucked out of nowhere, out of one of the abysses that has rutted out her brain. In our defense, some of us are horrified at what we have overlooked during these conversations.

(How could Ruth do that to a child?)

In Ruth's defense, Silla sounded pretty when she whispered it. Sibilant, like the wind threading itself through the branches right before the cradle burst. She imagined confetti, a party of color swirling silently in the air in the space where the cradle and the baby had been.

Don't forget:

Adah, who was born with eleven fingers. Regan, raped into silence. Helen, who can't speak because she won't.

Mara, who was Godless.

When the message, laden with its Gods-this and Gods-that and heavy with the weight of Ruth, reached Mara at the hotel she'd taken for her team members and herself near the center of S_____, Mara simply folded it in two and paid the man at the desk who'd taken it down for his time and his generosity with the words. Ruth must have tracked her through the department, not knowing it would be an impossible task to find her.

The air was wet and Mara thought she could smell her own odor, although after two months out in the middle of nowhere, she was probably way beyond that. Her skin felt as though it had curdled and clumped along her bones, and her hair when she let it go from its greasy ponytail clung to her shoulder blades like webbing. She'd walked through countless webs over the past two months and never complained, but in that room with her own body catching her in its sticky strands, she wiped a palm frantically across her face, across the memory of silk catching along her eyelashes and getting into her mouth.

She scrubbed herself in the meager drip of the shower, and when she finished, the floor at her feet was streaked with mud and littered with crumbled bits of leaf and branch and who knows what—insect wing, eggshell, flossy remnants of fur and bone. Detritus from the world she'd exited only hours before. It was amazing how quickly reality could disassemble itself and re-form into some other reality. She counted things as she dried herself—welts, bites, ribs, missing pints of blood (estimated)—the forest already a murky spot of some emotion.

The curtains had been pulled when she entered, and the room was warm and dim. Mara laid a clean towel across the bed and sat naked on it and stared at the wall for several minutes before she remembered. She reached for her pile of clothes on the floor and pulled the note from the pocket of her crusted pants and lay back on the bed, her hair soaking the flat pillow. She read it in the stark yellow light from the single bulb above her. She could forget how early it was under that light. She planned to sleep for at least sixteen hours.

What was in that note? We could pontificate for hours (and often do), but only three people in the world know for sure: Mara, Ruth, and the gentleman at the front desk. And maybe even Ruth doesn't know, since it was transferred to Mara via a bilingual, international, Russian-roulette game of telephone.

'Could the man speak English?' Jessica, who gave her virginity to Paul Deacon (Paul Deacon!), demands. "Because did he even translate it right?' 'Well, Mara came home,' Shelly says. 'So he got something right.' 'Unless Ruth didn't want Mara to come back,' Naomi says, but no one ever listens to Naomi because she says the dumbest things, and at the sound of her own voice, she blushes and goes still. Movement means we might remember that she has spoken.

Honestly, it makes us think of things locked in ocean depths. Of tentacles undulating under a slow fall of sediment that winks briefly as it passes through the last of whatever is left of the light.

SilllaaAHHH.

Who is Ruth? Well, it's probably obvious. Ruth is the crazy-ass one.
The one with the bad ovaries. The one who never had a boyfriend.

136

The one who heard people talking behind her even when she was a teenager and would look around at all the wrong times and never was able to catch them at it and so interpreted the voices as angels. The one who believed that God would find a reason and a way for her to be a mother because wasn't that one of God's particular skill-sets? Not the rationalizing of it—that was not a skill reserved for deities - but the making of virgins into mothers. No one Ruth knew personally had managed that trick. Scientists maybe, with tweezers and piles of frozen eggs, inserting them one by one between the legs of virgins, but that she counted as trickery, and anyway, they weren't often virgins by then. Not really. What God could do would be called a miracle.

Sixteen hours.

But the message from Ruth had wormed down through Mara's gray matter and left sinuous tunnels behind it, and Ruth emerged from these tunnels with webs for hair and soft iridescent wings where her ears might otherwise be, and when she opened her mouth, a tongue long and slender as a proboscis spilled out and with it unfurled words that Mara couldn't remember when she woke seven hours after tumbling into that deafening sleep.

She tried to go back to sleep now that it was dark beyond her window, but her internal clock was wound in strange ways—maybe too tightly, maybe was now steadily ticking backwards through time—and she finally rolled onto her stomach and pressed her face into the pillow and made a sustained, muffled, guttural sound that might have been the word *fuuuucckk*. Or possibly it was *Ruuuttthhh*. At any rate, after the sound was released, she got up and put on a pair of underwear still damp from its bath in the sink and the cleanest of her filthy clothes and she went down the stairs and pushed at the heavy door that opened onto the street.

There was right and there was wrong, and Mara didn't need a god to tell her what was what. Ruth, even though she apparently had God whispering in her ear most of the time, still couldn't seem to grasp the differences. It was why Mara preferred the forest. Any forest. Anywhere that Ruth wasn't. Anywhere that Ruth's God wasn't. Although Ruth would say that wasn't possible.

The street wasn't empty. Light spilled from windows, and voices collapsed out of the doorways of bars and restaurants like dust and debris from unheard detonations. There was a large park in the middle of town with colored fountains and groups of people playing music and strolling in pairs and clusters and selling food and buying each other cheap bracelets and earrings and sitting on dirty benches and cavorting in the damp grass. If Mara went right, she'd wind up in the middle of all this. To the left was mostly darkness, the road winding up and out of sight and only a streetlight or two illuminating the doorways of closed shops. As long as she stood on the single step that popped out of the hotel doorway like a stubby tongue she still had options.

Of course she went left. (We feel we could have predicted it.) She was tired, and left was the territory of instinct. No decisions would have to be made if she went left. Going left meant that action would happen or not happen. When you realize that a jaguar is stalking you, you don't waste time reviewing your options.

A man on the other side of the street stepped off the curb and approached, raising his hand to her. She pointed at him (instinct!), her own arm outstretched.

"Back the fuck off."

And he lowered his hand and retreated. She wondered which part of her response had affected him.

Mara walked. She walked to tire herself out, but that didn't happen. It was a small city, and the streets wound in and out and formed themselves into knots and stars, but her sense of direction had been so well-honed in the forest that even now she couldn't seem to get lost. No matter what, she kept coming back to the glittering central park.

In a doorway not far from the park but after a turn so that it was quiet and lit only glimmeringly, sat three boys and a small girl. The boys were young, but not so young that they weren't already nearly Mara's height. They rose as she passed, and she knew they were following her before they spoke. One of them leaped forward and tapped her on the shoulder, and her heart began to push more firmly against her blood. They began to talk about how pretty she was but the words they used meant something else.

Something struck her between the shoulder blades. A fragment of bottle glass or a pebble. She made an effort to keep walking at a steady pace. She'd dealt with this type of harassment before. They'd get bored and head off to the park where there were plenty of tourists who would scare more easily. Or at least more visibly.

Something hit her upper arm and clicked against her watch, a tiny sound that drew her fear up into her throat. She turned and bore down on them. They scrambled down the street, but she kept after them furiously. "I don't have any money," she said in their language. "I'm tired. I'm fucking tired, and I have nothing you want. Nothing. Alright? You goddamn little fuckers!"

Near the doorway where she'd found them, they stopped, and she slowed as she approached. The light from the park fell dimly across their faces, and she saw that they really were only children. Wild-haired, dirty boys swaddled in threadbare sweatshirts and broken shoes. The little girl held the hand of one of them and glared at Mara, and it was those eyes that pierced her rattling armor and released some of the pressure of her anger.

"Why are you following me?" she asked.

They didn't answer, but neither did they move away from the doorway. It was their castle, and she was preventing them from retreating to its parapets. "If you want money," she said, "I don't have any on me. I don't know what else you want, unless you're just trying to scare people."

One of the boys shook his head slightly. "No, ma'am," he said.

"Your parents teach you that? Following people around in the dark just to be assholes?"

"No, ma'am," he said.

"It's late," she said. "It's night. Why aren't you at home?"

The same boy crossed his arms and glanced down at the little girl. "My papa," he said. "He in Florida or something, I don't know. My mama out with some *pendejo* somewhere, probably, I don't know."

Mara had heard these types of truths before from other street children, and even from some of the men who she'd taken with her into the forest to help carry her private things and her cases of specimens.

"Well. I don't think you belong here," she said. And finally: "Have you eaten today?"

The boy with the whore for a mother uncrossed his arms and pulled his sleeves down over his hands, and the others did nothing. "Alright," Mara said. "Alright, you little thieves. I'm going to buy you dinner in the park." But the little girl continued to glare at her, and so —following her instinct again—Mara lunged at her, baring her teeth, her hands spread as if to grab the girl. The boys jumped, their feet stuttering on the sidewalk, but the girl remained expressionless. Mara drew back and pushed her fingers through her hair to remove it from her eyes. It felt heavy and greasy again. Someone else's hair.

"Come on," she said wearily.

And they followed, the girl lagging behind with her arms crossed over her flat little ribcage. Mara could feel the girl's eyes on her, and it was like the husk of a butterfly had been pinned at the base of her neck. Her spine felt tight, as though the connective tissue had dried out and the vertebrae sucked up against each other. It took a great amount of effort to not turn around.

How old was this girl? No more than eight years old. No more than seven.

Even so, it's hard for us to picture her anywhere else.

Not much later, Mara fell onto the bed. Light leaked through a crack between the curtains and onto the clothes she'd thrown across a wooden chair, slumping from there to the stained and faded pattern on the tiled floor. They'd be hungry again tomorrow, she thought. But that was the way it was. The children themselves hadn't seemed upset by, or even cognizant of, the unsustainable precariousness of their lifestyle. She slept, and when the sun came up, she woke for the second time in that room and picked up Ruth's letter.

Ruth didn't say it exactly, but it was clear to Mara that she had somehow wound up with a baby that wasn't hers. It was the God references—the miracles sprinkled throughout—the knowledge that Mara had of Ruth in the first place. Ruth, who had always been at best half-in and half-out of whatever world Mara inhabited at any given moment. Ruth who had terrible ovaries.

The message must have revealed at least two additional facts because later Mara knew the baby's name, although she forgot that it was temporary (whatever that meant). *I'm calling her Sara. That's just temporary, though. She doesn't cry. She really doesn't cry. She's such a quiet baby.*

And it must have said, in one way or another: *Come back.* Because Mara went to the airport that afternoon, begrudgingly, burdened with cases of insects and boxes of notebooks whose pages had become glued together with mold and bags of clothes heavy with dirt and sweat and parts of the forest and with a slight ache in her spine and with all her old, complicated feelings about Ruth.

Mara, who would have rather left Ruth to her demons. Mara, upon who it now befell the task of rescuing a child she had never met. Returning it and Ruth to their rightful places in the world.

But she went, didn't she, and we all have our opinions about that.

The clouds pile in over the trees. Someone—Penny, maybe, who has tanned herself to leather over the years (who has been a lover of light, burnished like the coin she's named for by thousands of hours of sun reflected seductively from myriad oceans) - thinks to start the fires. We have planned to make a few fires. Hundreds or thousands of fires. Fires like armies of stars falling across our patch of earth.

We go out to collect wood, returning in the gloaming as spiky, monstrous silhouettes, piles of branches balanced strangely on our heads and fanned menacingly over our shoulders like clustered lances, so that we look like inhuman conquistadoras marching through vast nations in search of places to let fall our burdens. In search of palaces and fountains and sources of steel. Things to ravish and hoard.

Now we've set into place a universe that descends as the clouds do. Flames lift and the world presses them back down over us. That canopy of light sparkles off Nina's hand—Nina, who can never just wait for shit—when she offers it to us for our approval. (And what can we do but approve?) It sparkles off the soda cans mounded into coolers like chests of jewels, and the metal webbed painfully through Gabby's mouth, and the *Angel* spelled out in rhinestones that curves prettily across Kelly's ass.

What do we discuss as we're warming our hands over these fires? What else? Ruth, who has remade herself into something loved. Mara, who has remade herself into something necessary.

Mara finds the right door. One of the numbers is gone, but she can read the shadow of it in the faded paint, and she has a brief fantasy wherein she rears her leg back and smashes the door flat with the sole of her boot and rushes in to save the faceless infant Sara. Wherein she ends the emotionally turbulent Saga of Ruth forever. The air is cool, but the sun is incendiary and washes out the motel so that it looks overexposed and sterile. Inexplicably it reminds Mara of the forest (any forest)—the benevolence of its leaves, the dirty exuberant squabbling of its inhabitants and the bright splash of their other noises, and its cool, lush darkness. Mostly that.

Mara raises her hand, knots her fingers into a loose fist, and then notices that the door is open. Just a crack—not even enough to let light into the room beyond. She releases the fist and pushes at the door with both hands, her fingertips fanned the way you might hold them if you were about to catch something bulky and difficult to handle. Like a beach ball. Or an infant that has been sent tumbling through the air.

Ruth has just scissored through a chunk of her own hair. When Mara enters, spilling great gobs of light through the dimness, Ruth turns from the mirror at the back of the room and freezes, although Mara doesn't understand what part of this Ruth didn't expect.

"You left the door open," Mara says. The first words she has spoken to Ruth in how many years? Four? Ruth looks older and, even with the scissors dangling from her fingers and sheathed as she is in a glittering nimbus comprised of particles of hair released from her body into the sunlight, she looks absolutely, completely sane. All her angels appear to have deserted her for how normal she looks. She doesn't look like a virgin or a person who would think to steal a baby from a car. She doesn't look like Ruth at all.

Two beds separate Mara and Ruth. The baby, Sara, is lying on her back in the middle of the bed closest to the door.

"I assume you're here to take her," Ruth says. "Even though she's my daughter."

"Oh Jesus, Ruth. Sara is someone else's daughter, remember?"

"Her name is Silla," Ruth says, and for a moment, Mara is disoriented. How many babies has Ruth taken? "I don't know what the other mother called her," Ruth says. "But I've been calling her Sara so no one can find us." Ruth drops her hair into the sink and Mara's brain settles itself. Typical Ruth, making changes to obscure that which no one could identify in the first place. Cutting off hair no one has ever seen. Changing the baby's name when the only name that matters is the one Ruth doesn't even know.

The baby moves her mouth thoughtfully, dimpling at something up near the ceiling, and a bubble of spit forms between her pursed lips. Maybe she, too, has angels putting words and names into her head. Mara wonders what the baby's (real) name is. Can you have more than one? But the way in which Ruth has always been consistent is that she has never spoken a lie. Ruth always tells the truth as she knows it.

Ruth says: "Look, I'm fully aware of what I'm supposed to do, Mara. I know why you're here. You don't understand me, but I understand you." She turns to place the scissors carefully onto the counter, and Mara can see her hair pulled back into a jagged nub, the remains of a long ponytail.

When she turns back, she's crying. "I think she belongs with me," Ruth says. "I do. But you don't, and I don't know what that means."

Mara thinks of the little girl glaring on the dark street in S_____, and she tries to think generously about the emotional state of the baby's (real) mother, and she tries to avoid wondering what might happen if she just lets herself believe in the truth as Ruth knows it. Mara is closer to the child, but only by a few steps. Ruth, she supposes, could move fast enough to get there first, now that she's not weighed down by the scissors. Now that she's removed the weight of her own hair.

"The only thing I know is that this is my daughter," Ruth says. She takes a step towards the baby on the bed. One step. And then the baby makes a sound, and the bubble at her lips bursts, an audible pop in the quiet room. She takes a startled breath. Her face shrivels, and Mara and Ruth look away from each other and stare at the child whose skin has reddened like the blush of nature endangered, who is now pudgy and creased and damp as a cupid.

The baby wails, and sunlight floods into the room from the open door.

We've already said it, but we'll happily repeat it ten thousand times: Our fires are beautiful. There are hundreds of them, thousands of them, like a diamond necklace has been torn open and splashed into the trees and into the clotted dark roots of the meadow. The light moves across the remnants of our picnic—plastic bowls emptied and glistening with juice pooled in the bottoms, berry-stained tablecloths, bottles and cans glittering and spilling from gleaming black trash bags tacked up onto trees, plastic wrap draped over dark mounds of leftover meat sparkling with grease—and illuminates us.

But what about Ruth and Mara? What about Silla? Or Sara? Or whoever she is, if she is in fact someone else.

'Well, I guess...' Lila says, and many of us nod encouragingly, if cryptically. Lila, the one with the eyes as blue as glacial ice that give her the distracted, distant air of a saint, as though she can't really make out our features, blinks several times and looks up. And what does she see? Faces emerging from the darkness, parts of us emerging and diverging back into the flickering night. We sisters, illuminated, standing still among the glittering detritus of our picnic.

'She had to go and pick up the baby. I mean, she had to. She couldn't just leave a baby crying there like that on the bed.' Lila wipes inelegantly at her nose and says, 'Right?'

But in the dark with its tumbling shadows that make bulbous the pretty noses and lengthen cropped hair and slim the fat girls into waifs and thicken the thighs of the waifs, you really couldn't say with any certainty that Lila still had saints' eyes. You wouldn't be able to say what color they were at all.

John Hoppenthaler
THE GARDEN OF EDEN
—New City, NY, 1965

He placed one looped end of a thin, white rope
between her ring and middle finger,
closed her hand over it, then walked away

with the other end until the line pulled taut.
Soon, wash appeared. A billowing sheet.
Boxer shorts, her camisoles. A flutter

of colorful shirts & water-heavy blue jeans,
cuffs nearly grazing the dusty grass.
He built a suitable fence around the yard.

Then they were both free to roam the property,
& the one sunny corner, & they made
a garden of it. Nothing fancy. Rows

of lettuce, carrots, parsley & melons.
He put up another fence—wire mesh
to bedevil hungry deer—but the two of them

passed easily in & out of the gate. Soon
honeysuckle covered the fence & drenched
morning air with bees and sweetness, & soon

tomato plants arose, & together they staked them.
Then aphids & a compost pile. & debt
began to appear, credit cards, a mortgage,

& then shirts faded, & underwear grew threadbare,
& wild thoughts began to enter their heads.
Still the garden thrived. Together they pinched

suckers, weeded & watered. When the slug jars
needed refilling, each would pour a few sips
from beers they held in their hands as sunlight

arced away into dusk. It couldn't be said
that times weren't tough, but they ate often
from the garden. Weather rarely let them down.

They weren't religious, but it pleased them to think
of that other garden. They'd come to see themselves
as whom you'd already guessed, & had gained

all the knowledge they'd ever need, as they saw it.
"It" being the gradual process of growing
old while their children gorged themselves on the ripest fruit.

John Hoppenthaler

IMMIGRANT SONG

"Das ist kein Amerika," my mother told me
Uncle Eddie would say after just a few weeks

in Jersey, *"Das ist Fehlerika!" Ein Fehler*—mistake—
land of mistake. Bad decision. Error. Misstep.

Wrong turn. Dead end. Comma
splice. Run on sentence. Fumble

words—the ball. Drop the ball;
drop the night class. Wrong bus. Wrong

stop. Wrong neighborhood. Wrong country.
Failure. *Ein Fehler. "Das ist kein Amerika."*

My uncle died young, a mistake.
He made an error and he died.

Toni Mirosevich

SHOTGUN

I grew up in a shotgun house. Open the front door and it was a straight shot through the front room, through the kitchen, the bedroom, the bath, before a bullet—or a gust of wind—hit the back wall of the house, came out the other side, and continued past the patio, the swing set, one swing still vibrating from the last ringing ride, past the clothesline, the cherry tree, past the backyard fence, right through the bull's eye knot in the fence's knotted pine to enter the neighbor's yard. From there it was anyone's guess when the bullet would finally find a wall, tree, body to meet its journey's end.

Or maybe it was called a shotgun because my father had a shotgun hidden in the closet, like in that old sing along song, "She Wore A Yellow Ribbon," which he'd sing every time he'd had a few. I knew the lyrics by heart: *Behind the door her father kept a shotgun, he kept it in the springtime and in the month of May, hey, hey! And if you ask him why the heck he kept it, he kept it for her lover who was far, far away.*

But I wasn't the one with a lover far, far away. I was just a kid growing up in a very narrow house. It was my father who was far, far away most nights, far away from home, but maybe not that far, maybe just down the block.

When his nights out began to multiply his excuses began to grow like pearls on a necklace, each pearl a perfect round excuse, polished and shining in the moonlight. It wasn't long before the single strand grew to a double strand: He'd tell us he'd been at the movie theatre, holed up with his best friend who ran the projector, but what could those two be doing up there in the blackened projection room, smoking in silence as night after night they watched the same film roll by? He'd say he'd been at the bowling alley, helping his nephew set up the pins, and then tell us how long it took, after every strike, to set each wobbling pin upright again. He'd say he was down at the church, meeting with the other men in the Holy Names Society, all who had promised to not take the name of the Lord in vain.

When we pushed and asked more specific questions he said he'd told us enough. He said he was either there or there or there or somewhere else.

It was left up to my mother to decide if each pearl was real or a fake. She bit down hard on one pearl, then another. They crumbled like sugar cubes. So she hired a private detective to tail him, to find out where he went to, where he whiled away his time.

When the detective came up with the goods, the visual proof that there was another, my mother couldn't bear to see my father, 'caught with his pants down,' as a neighbor lady might say, so she sent me in her stead. I was to take the bus down to the seedy part of town, near the stockyards where the cattle bellowed and moaned that the end of the world was near.

One day, after school, still wearing my school uniform—my plaid pleated skirt, my white dickey, my polished loafers, my circle pin—I showed up at the detective's office. A man in a rumpled shirt, suspenders, and wrinkled slacks, a cigarette dangling from his lips—just like the private eyes in the gangster movies my father told me about—opened the office door and asked me to have a seat. He pulled black and white photographs out of a manila folder and placed them on the green blotter on his desk. I looked close and saw a man who looked like my father in a series of movie stills, as if he was an actor auditioning to play a part. He had his arms wrapped around a woman with blonde curly hair. She was wearing a black slip and her eyes were closed like she was sleeping. Maybe he was whispering something into her ear. Maybe she'd forgotten her lines. Maybe he was telling her all the words he could no longer say now that he was a member of the Holy Names Society.

When I brought the evidence home my mother took the folder and without opening it to look inside, walked into the kitchen pantry, pulled out the potato bin and slipped it behind the bin, into the dark space where sometimes we heard little nibbling sounds.

* * *

That night, as it grew late, as the darkness inside gathered in the corners of the house, under the beds, in the closet with the shotgun, in the folds of my mother's yellow apron and the darkness outside gathered in the front yard, crept up the porch steps, seeped under the front door and flowed over the living room carpet, my mother turned to me, and said,

"Let's go climb into bed. We'll wait together."

I followed her into *their* bedroom and climbed into *their* great white boat of a bed, so much bigger than the small skiff of a bed in my own damp room.

We lay there, pretending to sleep but not sleeping. The night came and went, came and went, for the bedroom window faced the main road. Every time a car passed by headlights hit the window and, for an instant, the bedroom would become as bright as day before plunging us into night again.

"Is it him this time?" I'd ask as each day sped past. "No, maybe next time," she'd answer, for she knew his headlights. They were as recognizable to her as a birthmark or a person's walk. To me his headlights seemed larger than those of other cars, like full moons or suns or planets. The light they cast was more golden than yellow. Sometimes his headlights looked like the klieg lights used to announce a store's *Grand Opening*, that shot up into the night and crisscrossed. Sometimes they looked like gold pick-up sticks tossed across the ceiling's sky.

Minutes passed, then hours. Lights filled and emptied the room. The cycle of days and nights began to slow, then stopped altogether. Now it was pitch black like the darkness you'd find inside an unopened oyster shell—complete, total—the type of darkness needed to grow a pearl or an excuse.

I looked at the alarm clock on the bedside table. It was way past my bedtime. It was past all the bedtimes of the world. My mother saw me notice the time then turned to me and said,

"Let's make a house with our feet. I'll start."

Under the covers, she began to move her right foot.

"Here," she said, "First, let's make the footprint of the house," and laughed at that small joke. On the bottom sheet, she drew the perimeter of a house with her big toe, a square as big as the Big Houses on the Hill, where the rich people lived, with their porch columns, Ionic or Doric or the other kind.

"This is the living room," she said, and sketched out a large square within the perimeter's square; no tunnel-shaped house, no shotgun this. She drew three large picture windows instead of one single small front window like we had in our living room, where we placed the Christmas tree or, in the offseason, a potted plant.

"Hop on board," she said so I took my foot and placed it on hers. I held on with my toes. I followed her feet to see where they went to next. I let myself be led.

"Here," my mother said, as she marked out a small rectangular shape. "Here's where the sofa will be. What kind of fabric do you think we should use? What about a rose brocade?" And we both began to draw the small swirls of the brocade, then the tassels that hung off the sofa's skirt.

"Look, here's where we'll put the fireplace and here's the front door. How about a Dutch door with a top half that swings out?" I felt the little swinging motion she made with her toe and followed along. We both swung out together, we both rode that swing. I pictured the neighbor ladies popping their heads in the opened top half of that door, coming by for the Come As You Are parties they sometimes held on mornings when they all were bored. Mrs. Brewer would drop by in her shower cap and robe. Mrs. Scott, in her slip and curlers, would shout, "You caught me with my pants down," and all the ladies would laugh.

"Now you," my mother said.

I took my big toe and started to draw a line then stopped. I was nervous. I'd never built a house before. Where should I begin? I decided to start with a room that would please my mother.

"Here's the kitchen," I said and with my toe I made a nice sized room and then drew a fancy stove with six burners, not like our old model with the broken stove light. I drew a kitchen table with three chairs. I drew new cupboards. I began to feel like I was getting the hang of it. I put a copper pan on the stove and a nice stew pot on to boil. When I began drawing the cubed potatoes and carrots in the stew my mother said, "Now, let's not get too specific."

The rooms began to grow. Who was going to stop us now? Who would say no to our dreamy floor plan? Why stop at two bedrooms? Why not have three or four and a second bathroom, a full daylight basement, a swimming pool?" "I want a stable," I said. Every Christmas morning my father greeted me by saying, "I got you a horsey but he runned away," so I build the stalls and put in a Palomino, a Pinto pony and some thoroughbreds. I let the horses out to pasture and our feet galloped across the bed.

Before long, the house grew from a large rancher to a large split-level to a mansion. The bottom sheet was covered with additions and new wings and a two car garage.

When we were done with the inside we tiptoed out the front door and landscaped the yard. We put in full grown oaks, box hedges, roses in bloom, an herb garden, then a sweeping driveway, an apple orchard. We would have kept going but the edge of the bed stopped our land grab.

It was exhausting, all this building, and I was starting to get sleep. I knew I'd fall off the edge soon and before I did I wanted to lift up the covers to see our grand new house, to see the world we'd made.

I lifted the blankets. It was dark under there, so dark I couldn't make out the rooms. When I complained my mother cried out, "Oh no! I forgot to pay the electric bill!"

The one thing we needed was light. It was the only thing we'd forgotten to create.

"How do you draw light?" I asked.

My mother thought we could bring candles up from the basement— but first we'd need to draw the basement, then the shelves that held the candles and then the candles themselves. We set to work on making the basement stairs and then walked down them. While we were down there we put up some can goods on the shelves for the long, cold winter ahead.

All of the sudden there was a flash of light. A burst. A flood. Bigger than a thousand suns. Bigger than a thousand moons. Underneath the covers all the rooms in our house lit up like the Titanic before it turned upright and slid into the dark, dark sea. Every window, every staircase, every archway glowed and you could make out the finest details of all we made.

The house went dark in a snap. As quickly as the light came it was gone.

"Maybe a circuit blew," I said. My mother's feet stopped moving. Then I heard the key in the front door. I heard the doorknob turn. I heard the front door open. A sharp cold gust blew in, a straight shot that passed through the front room, the kitchen, the bedroom, passed beneath the bed covers and blew out the candles we'd forgotten to light.

Ekphrasis Poems
by Richard Jackson

Photo by Richard Jackson

Richard Jackson
HOURGLASS

All that's left of history is disposition, as Lorenzetti knew,
his Temperance holding an hourglass as if to show
a way of practicing death again and again. We were
brought here to be taken away, she says. Did the shore
provoke the wave? the broken branch the wind?
Beside the abandoned house a rusted swing set
with not swings. We try to position ourselves inside
the narrow now, away from acid throwing terrorists,
Mali rebels, and assault rifles next door. Promise
gives way to simple measure of what is not. The hunched
woman at the checkout, she knows. Still, the water meter
gets read, the car filled, the groceries bought, while
our unlived lives sift back and forth through time.

Photo by Richard Jackson

Richard Jackson

THE DANCING BUILDING, PRAGUE

There is no one shape for truth. It used to be
you could see it in the outline of a winter tree
against the sky. Now the pigeons carry bits of broken
dreams away, the windows fill with questions
we never hear. In one room an artist fails to paint
his ghosts, in another a clerk keeps erasing his own
name. Sooner or later an answer leans over to whisper.
One time it was 1954, the rapids twisting down
the flume. What did it matter if we didn't understand?
It was about balance. It was about the way sunlight,
for one irretrievable moment, makes everything dance.
A truth caught with its mouth open. The sky tilting
away forever. It is like imagining the dead visit you
and then mistake you, they believe this, for one of them.

Photo by Richard Jackson

Richard Jackson

VOLUNTEERS

for Terri

It was our belief that all roads lead somewhere
that was our downfall. In fact, everyone was leading
a life hidden from themselves. Meteors skim by,
stars explode, graveyards are grown over. I struggle,
now, just to describe the smell of rain on asphalt
that still carries me, after all these years, to a place
I can't indentify. There was a boy back then burned
from fresh road tar. Another who fell from the roof
we used to climb. I still can't figure out how they are
related. History takes care of itself despite our attempts
at revision. In the end it isn't hard to abandon truth's
training wheels. It's love, after all that takes us
where we want to go, and every love is more than
its love, like those *volunteers*, you call them, that grow
unexpectedly from seeds you buried in the compost,
arriving, as it were, from nowhere we needed to identify.

Photo by Richard Jackson

Richard Jackson

THE RAPIDS

The river we have inside us suspects the truth.
That Life began, as Lucretius said, by inheriting itself.
That everything just changed from one kind of atom
to another. This is a belief that Hypatia of Alexandria was
flayed alive for. Now the light thickens. The water is
deeper than it seems. We know what our words mean
by what flows over them. That's why they keep changing
before we can say them. Does the river remember
the rocks it grinds into sand? The shape of the river is
a question asked miles upstream. Language is fossil poetry,
wrote Emerson. What was left of the famous library
in Alexandria was burned by Calef Omar. No one knows
what happened to the 113 lost plays of Sophocles.
Sometimes, though, you can hear what the river has
brought to us. When we try to fathom any of this we are
talking about the depth of two outstretched arms,
about six feet, or about the average depth Of a grave.
This is why the first philosophy, as they say, was about
indigestion. *To Philosophize is to learn to die*, wrote Montaigne.

Photo by Richard Jackson

Richard Jackson

FAITH IN ROMANIA

It must be the child has turned to call us to follow.
The cart is filled with the harvest. Ahead of them
The road can't decide between harvest and planting.
The camera has refused to read an invisible dust
That rises like prayer. They are headed towards mounds
That are man's early attempts to reach heaven.
A hidden road turns left. Not yet dusk but already
The stars are waiting to drink the darkness.
My gaze here stumbles through lost centuries.
The early moon behind me pretends it is a clock.
They could be heading to Emmaus or Egypt.
What they seek is what we find in them.
We are all prisoners of our own happiness.

Joel Smith
THE PRESSURE PRINCIPLE

E-book or no E-book, Stella was done with guerilla camping. That summer, she and Gabers had pioneered a new kind of European grand tour. Starting with the Tour Eiffel, they'd spent a night at every tourist attraction in the E.U. There'd been that balcony by the Tower of London, the scaffolding overlooking La Sagrada Familia. And wherever they'd stayed, Stella and Gabers had written a chapter, passing her knockoff moleskine back and forth under the LED glow of his headlamp.

But sex on the ground, even when you're looking up at the ceiling of the Sistine Chapel, is still sex on the ground. And of course, her editor knew that section was going to be a forgery anyway, since in some places, security was just too tight.

"This is it Stel, the Galerie de Glaces, the Hall of Mirrors. It's the perfect climax for your book, infinite recursive lovemaking."

Gabers' rant broke Stella's thought train, and brought her back to Versailles, their last stop, back to Paris, where they'd started the loop one month before. Though she knew his features by heart, Stella took the opportunity to check Gabers out in one of the 357 mirrors that gave the arcade its name.

With that Roman nose—broken a dozen times in his skateboarding days—and those tattooed sleeves clasped behind his back in thought, Gabers could have been the court jester for Louis Quatorze.

"The fucking climax, babe, all chandeliers and opulence. Powdered wig orgies, you know?"

Stella turned from Gabers' reflection to her own, and felt lesser than, generic, a placeholder.

Gabers seized on Stella's distraction and stuck his hand down her convertible travel capris, drumming her butt to the Marseillaise. With his other hand he pulled a gold lamé bed sheet out of his messenger bag.

"A la Française, Artois, that's how we do."

"Call me a beer just one more time." Stella pulled his hand out of her pants, holding it like a defrosted mouse she was about to feed Sasha, their rainbow boa, back in Oakland.

"Hey, you get to call me Gabers, it's only fair."

"Look, let's just get behind the curtain and wait until dark, over there next to the bronze rooster."

"Fuck you, Stella, you know this was your idea. Don't resent me for making it happen." It was a tired argument, and they both knew it. Stella walked over to a Venetian Window (the sign called it a Venetia Window), and she drew the curtain behind her. It was the color of week-old Charles Shaw.

"Let's get caught then, Gabriel Surrey-Wheaton, excuse me, Gabriel Surrey-Wheaton the Third, last scion in a long line of douchebags."

"Okay, I'll summon the gardien, if that's what you want." Gabers had a smirk on; he never could resist himself. "And then I'll ask Monsieur Gardien if he wants to join in. We should do the Eiffel Tower right, we really should."

And in his best hammed up Douglas Fairbanks, Gabers swept himself behind the curtain, where Stella let him in.

Some time later, Stella awoke to a gentle cane in her side that she first thought was Gabers' night wood. No, they were most definitely busted. She tried to raise a hand in self-defense, but her arms had fallen asleep, pinned under Gabers' long ribcage.

A crusty janitor now loomed above them; he was old with nose hairs connecting to his moustache. Stella imagined that inside his cane was a rapier he used to skewer thieves and trespassers. She wondered how they could contact the American embassy, now that two Americans had been caught fucking on the National Patrimony of France, in the very room where The Great War ended. She wondered, half-serious, if the guillotine was still en vogue.

By now, Gabers had woken up too, though he seemed content to watch them all in the mirrors across the way. The old gardien seemed to inspect the situation at hand, from the gold lamé sheet to Stella's dead arm, and he laughed the laugh of a lifelong gauloise smoker.

"I use take my wife here at night, like you, and say, I am king, and she say me, then listen to you queen."

Pressing his cane to the floor to steady himself, the old man reached out to Stella, and kissed her hand as he pulled her up, leaving Gabers to rise on his own. He led them back to his closet, where the only light was the blue flicker of a butane stove. He motioned for them to sit on the floor and he put a pot of espresso on. Stella could see her and Gabers' faces in the angled stainless steel of the Morenita espresso maker. When it started whistling, she looked to Gabers, who had a comment waiting. He always had a comment waiting.

"It's the pressure principle, that's what makes it taste so damn good."

Joan Siegel

GAYHEAD

Summer of the first moon landing
I went swimming in the chill
Atlantic off Martha's Vineyard just beneath
clay cliffs where long ago

native Wampanoag sent their children
to harvest clay among rampant
poison ivy so in time they'd grow
resistant to its poison.

      I swam far out as fog wheeled over
waves shrouding me in opacity   purblind
I could not find my way   fighting
a riptide towing me farther   knowing

how twists of fate mark our time here
what if Apollo missed its rendezvous   Eagle
cut loose free-floating forever   no souls
of dead Wampanoag children to ferry us all home.

Kim Lozano

TAMPON DISPENSER
for JL

In the girls' bathroom of our school
the silver box hung there like it owned the place.
As invincible as an iron sink in a prison cell,
its fascist presence demanded we be women now,
its pink and aqua pictures insisted
we were supposed to like it.
When the door opened you could see it
from the hallway, and at the drinking fountain
the boys snuck peeks at that chamber
full of the strange little plungers
they'd examined in their mom's vanities.
They wanted to know what went on beyond that door
but were scared of getting too close,
to that room, and that box,
stainless steel, impregnable—forever an alien ship.

Liz Warren-Pederson

A REVERIE

> "The worst part of being single is being alone."
> — Drew Barrymore

Robin got to the park a full two hours before three o'clock, which was when her sister and the birthday girl were expected to arrive with the guests for the tea party. By that time, Robin's cabbage rose-printed dress would be mussed from carting box after box of party supplies and food from the back of her compact SUV over the little bridge to the park's pagoda-shaped ramada under the cherry trees.

Her SUV was parked illegally, with the hazards flashing, and there was a terrible moment when she realized she had to abandon the party supplies to drive partway around the block and properly park: when she was a girl, there had not been parking meters at the park, and now, returned home decades later, she was finding things much changed, least among them her younger sister's growing family, and the void left in the ancestral home now that her parents were gone. Once her mother would have thrown this party, but now it was her duty, the first duty of her return.

She rushed back to the ramada, half-expecting to find a group of cartoon hobos feasting on the mini cucumber sandwiches she'd cut out with a small, heart-shaped cookie cutter, guzzling decaffeinated Red Zinger tea filched from her oversized coffee carafe, and poking their dirty fingertips in among the sweet organza pouches she'd filled with gumdrops and nonpareils for the children. She was relieved to find her supplies unmolested, but, with her watch showing half-past one and the pink fruits of her considerable handicrafts still neatly tucked in six office paper boxes, she was overcome by a wave of mingled anger and anxiety, that somehow she was expected to pull this party off, single-handedly, while her younger sister coaxed sausage curls out of little Rachel's limp blonde locks in a bathroom across town. Twenty-two children were expected — fifteen girls, aged seven to nine, and seven boys, including the birthday girl's eleven-year-old brother Mickey, whose presence Robin did not understand.

"Couldn't Ron take Mickey and his friends to play mini golf?" Robin had asked her sister Julie, but Julie did not think that the boys would be much out of place.

"Just get them a piñata and some squirt guns," she'd told Robin. "They'll amuse themselves."

The piñata Robin had chosen was in the shape of a giant teapot. She'd gasped when she found it in the party shop, but the surly teen behind the counter failed to appreciate how perfect it was for Rachel's themed party, and also categorically refused to bargain, which meant that Robin was forced to grit her teeth and pay thirty dollars for something she knew would be ripped asunder at the hands of the seven small sinners Julie had welcomed into their girlish pagoda with open arms.

Robin waded into the project of décor with fierce concentration. She twined six parallel lengths of crepe paper into great swathes to hang from beam to beam on the ramada, creating a private boundary that no unapproved person could cross. She hung a pastel bunting customized in honor of the special day with hand-lettered text outlined in silver glitter. She draped tables in tissue paper in gradated shades of pink. She set out platters, both sweet and savory, and unwrapped the two dozen vintage teacups she'd picked up at thrift stores and then scoured with Comet and doused with boiling water to properly disinfect them from whatever they'd picked up from previous owners.

Then, at last, she settled at the head of the lead table, using a cloth napkin to dab at her forehead. Sweat pooled under her breasts. She had narrowly avoided snapping off a gel tip and her right index finger pulsed warmly where the tip had threatened to dislodge the thin natural nail below. Her hands shook, but the party was beautiful, magical. She looked up, and saw Julie coming up the path, Rachel in tow. Mickey came along behind them, kicking at the grass and thuggishly twirling a baseball bat up and over in tight loops with a neat flick of his wrist.

Robin stood, smiling, to greet them. The birthday girl hung back, but Julie came up right away. She was wearing jeans and a t-shirt. "Wow," Julie said, "it looks amazing." She wrapped her arms around Robin and held on for a beat too long. "You really shouldn't have," she added, low. "She just wanted Peter Piper. Really." She drew back, and Robin shook her head in smiling disbelief. "Tell Auntie Robin how grateful you are," Julie said to Rachel, and Rachel said thank you, under her breath.

Most days, Rachel wore Mickey's hand-me-down slip-on Vans and shredded t-shirts, but she had a doll-like beauty in her dress and Mary Janes. "Oh, you sweet girl," Robin exclaimed and bent to give her a hug. When she straightened up, she saw that Rachel was staring at the bunting, bemused. Robin could not tell if she was overwhelmed by the sheer beauty of the spectacle that had been created for her, or if she hadn't been properly exposed to the feminine over the course of her eight years.

Then the others began arriving, mothers and daughters in shorts and flip-flops, with the occasional boy coming up alone, abandoned curbside by a drive-by parent not interested in experiencing the tiny perfect world of the party. Robin deployed the girls to two of the tables, siphoning off the boys before they could touch anything. Each was armed with a plastic pistol from the dollar store and directed outside of the tea party proper, to the grassy grounds beyond the pagoda. There they loitered in a loose knot, bored. The mothers gathered around a third table, where, to Robin's surprise, they produced a few bottles of wine and began filling up teacups for themselves. She was left to manage the girls, who sat blinking at each other, not sure whether they were permitted to eat, or talk. Or if there would be games.

Robin had expected Julie to take up that end of the party, though they'd never explicitly discussed it. She stood at the pagoda's midpoint, wearing her pink sunhat tipped over one eye, waiting for the party to coalesce into a good time. Why were the girls dressed so casually? Why did they stare at each other, like mutes? At one end of the ramada, the mothers were opening a second bottle of wine. At the other, the gift table was overflowing with garishly-wrapped presents. The boys, still idle in the field, sent Mickey as an emissary. He stood at the pink crepe paper border and said, "Aunt Robin, we're hungry."

She turned and stared at him. She'd prepared enough sandwiches for each of the little girls to have three. Each table also had a large plate of cookies to share. And there was a tiered birthday cake with fresh flowers, for later. She mentally reviewed her to-do list, but the only things pertaining to the boys were "dollar store squirt guns" and "piñata" and "they'll amuse themselves." She had, she thought, close to twenty dollars in her purse. Perhaps they could walk two blocks to the convenience store.

Julie approached with her teacup. "What is it?" she asked Mickey.

"We're hungry," he said.

Julie turned and took a tray of cookies off the nearest table. The girls at the table tracked the rising tray of cookies with wide eyes. "Here," Julie said, and Mickey jogged off with his bounty. The girls silently telegraphed shock and outrage amongst themselves.

"That's all I've got," Robin stage whispered to Julie.

"Oh," Julie said. "Well, we can go halvsies with the other table." The second table of girls registered this with unspoken consternation.

Robin leaned in confidentially. "They're not eating," she murmured. "Should we have games? And when do you think we should open the gifts?" Her hands had begun to sweat. "Oh!" she added. "I haven't taken any pictures yet." She rushed to her purse and came back with her camera. She saw one of the little girls, who'd come in a baseball cap instead of a straw boater or sunhat, reach out and tug at the shoulder bow on Rachel's dress. Rachel slapped her hand away. Robin lowered her camera. She ought to have taken photos of the space before the children arrived.

Julie reached out and put a hand on Robin's forearm. "It's fine," she said. "Why don't you go organize games with the boys. I'll take care of the girls."

It was a form of damnation, but Robin took her penance. She teetered across the field to the boys, pumps sinking into the grass. The cookies were gone. The silver platter she'd plated them on was lying on the path. "Hello, boys," she said.

"This is my Aunt Robin," Mickey said. The boys muttered greetings. "We're still hungry," he added to her.

"Well," she said, "who wants to go to the Quik Mart?" They perked up immediately. "Holster your weapons," she said, and the boys pushed the plastic guns into their pants. She led the way, triumphant, pausing at the ramada just long enough to grab her purse. The girls were talking, finally, though she was appalled to see a raspberry macaron arc over the centerpiece and strike another girl in the forehead. The girl jerked back in surprise, then laughed.

At the convenience store, Robin deputized the boys to choose a single beverage each plus a bonus item. The bonus items ranged from hot dogs to gum, with one boy selecting a comic book. Robin stood in line, and when her turn came, clapped her hands, and the boys swarmed around her, sliding their Icees and Cokes and Red Bulls onto the counter. The clerk rang everything through, and it exceeded Robin's double sawbuck budget, but there was no disappointing the now-lively faces surrounding her, and she reluctantly charged the transaction. Then it was back to the park, goodies in hand. At one point, a brown-haired boy piped up in thanks, and they all took up the cry, and their gratitude swelled around Robin and she felt good about the expense, that it had been worth it, and the unequivocal right thing to do.

Back at the park, the girls had been set loose from the ramada. They'd torn down some of the bunting and abandoned their shoes. There was considerable jealousy at the boys' largesse. Robin stared, aghast. It was bad enough that they didn't look like little ladies; they didn't act like them either. Julie came up. Her teacup of wine was either never tasted, or always filled. "Why don't you set up the piñata?" she said.

So Robin unearthed it from the final box, where she'd carefully packed it in tissue paper. It was heavy with Tootsie Rolls and Smarties and SweeTarts and miniature boxes of Nerds. It had a built-in ring at the top, through which she'd looped a heavy, cream-colored drapery tieback with two feet of bullion trim dangling from its end. The children – all of them – gathered around in awe as she held the teapot aloft. Mickey came dragging his baseball bat, eyes wide, and for the first time, Robin wondered if a traditional rope might have been a better approach. She cleared her throat and held the teapot out. "Everyone will need to line up," she said.

"Auntie Robin," Mickey said, "you can't hold it!" She had been afraid of that. "Wait here," he said, and he returned with a folding chair, which he dragged to the nearest cherry tree. He stood on the chair and held out a hand, and Robin transferred the drapery tieback into his care. He threw it over a lowish branch so that one end hung freely, and she tried not to think of how the tieback's fine fibers would inevitably shred on the wood. "Here," he said to Robin and she took the end. He demonstrated how she was meant to raise and lower the piñata according to her own whim, or in accordance with the skill level of the striker.

"Oh," she said.

"Stand back," he advised. Then he yelled, "Everybody line up!" And the children fell into a neat if uneven line. Robin shifted in her heels on the grass, pulling at her dress with one hand, conscious that she herself had become part of the pulley tableaux: suspended from the cherry tree, the charming paper teapot, held aloft by a well-dressed woman, her elegant fingers encircling the knot of drapery tieback, its elaborate bullion dangling almost to her knees. She was arguably the most essential part: the operator of the festive machinery.

Mickey had found something to blindfold the children. The first in line was a dark-haired child with pigtails. He tied the blindfold around her head, put the bat in her hands, spun her around three times, and aimed her at the piñata. Before he let her go, he turned back and addressed the entire group: "My turn is after Tommy." There were nods. He looked at Robin for final approval and she nodded solemnly. Then Mickey pushed the striker and she stumbled forward toward the piñata, poking rather than swinging, and confronted with this feeble display, Robin took pity and lowered the teacup directly into her path.

The bat connected with a tap Robin barely registered through the drapery tieback, and she watched in admiration as Mickey, already clapping, approached the girl. He took the bat right out of her hand, told her she'd done well, and sent her to the back of the line.

The next was one of his own friends, and Mickey tied the blindfold doubly tight and spun him around and around, shoving him forward so that he staggered like a drunk. Robin saw Mickey nod and knew that the lack of balance was unlikely to affect his swing, so she pulled the teapot up out of reach just as the bat sliced through the air. The children cheered and Robin grinned, lowering the teapot again for the second of what Mickey called out would be three tries. The bat connected on the last try, but it was a glancing blow, which set the piñata to wobbling unsteadily, still intact.

The game escalated as they began to work through the line a second time. Robin had kicked off her heels and tossed her hat on the grass. She heaved the piñata aloft and yelled "Hey, batter, batter" along with the children in mockery of whomever was striking. Someone zinged the handle off the teacup, which by then also had one dented side, and then the line arrived at Tommy, who was followed by Mickey, who was followed by a third boy of their age, all of whom had demonstrated a combination of ferocity and accuracy that seemed certain to obliterate the piñata. The line disintegrated as if on command, and the children gathered around Robin and the cherry tree and the teacup in anticipation of retrieving its sugary viscera. She tried to pull the teacup out of Tommy's way, but he anticipated her and swung high. The teacup rocked violently on the drapery pull and a few Tootsie Rolls tumbled out. There were shrieks of expectation, all around, and Mickey yelled for everyone to hold back until the piñata collapsed.

Then it was his turn, and Tommy blindfolded him. Mickey wiped his hands on his jeans several times before he took the bat from Tommy, then Tommy spun him around and around, and the children yelled things at him, and Robin yelled too, "Hey batter, batter," and "Hit it!" He reeled toward the piñata and there was a sudden hush, and Robin hesitated before she leaned back on the drapery pull, wondering if she'd become too obvious; if Mickey, like Tommy, had seen through her overly-simple strategy, and then she heaved back, shouting, and it might have been the extra shout that startled him, because then, as Mickey completed his swing, the bat whistled through the air, and kept whistling, sliding through his fingers and catapulting out into the circle of children, where they waited in anticipation of the teacup's explosion on the grass.

Time slowed, and to Robin the bat seemed to hang in the air, a sleek, silvery missile, and then it made contact with one of the girls, striking her in the mouth with a force that sent her reeling back. Someone screamed. The girl coughed and sat down hard on her butt in the grass, mouth open. Blood poured down her chin. One of her front teeth was jagged and black with blood. The second front tooth was either missing or too red with gore to register as a tooth. Robin stood holding the drapery tie, dumb with shock. More of the girls screamed. Mickey had torn off the blindfold and rushed to the girl's side. Several of the girls came to stand with Robin. They stared at her, eyes full of expectation, but she didn't know what it was that they expected from her.

Then the mothers were on the scene, taking control, organizing, calling out orders and suggestions, reining in the chaos: "Get some milk!" "Get Hope's mom on the phone!" "You! Bring me paper towels!" "Where's the closest dentist?" One of the mothers herded the more histrionic girls back off to the pagoda. Another was rocking toothless Hope. A third galvanized the boys to search for the tooth or teeth that had been knocked asunder and lost in the grass. Julie rushed by Robin, pausing long enough to tell her to drop the piñata and help look for the teeth. Robin released the drapery pull at once, and the teacup mushed on the ground, leaking candy at its weak points. No one noticed.

She fell in with the boys, crawling in the grass, but she wasn't so much looking for teeth as she was running her hands over the grass, which was damp and close-clipped from recent park maintenance, and a dark, deep green that a tooth would surely shine from. Her throat felt tight and her fingers shook, and she was grateful to have a task, a job to carry out in the all the confusion, and grateful to Julie for having given it to her: to be busy was a gift. Then Tommy cried out in victory and one of the mothers swooped in with a teacup of cream, and Julie picked up the crying, bloody-faced child and trekked across the park, Tommy following behind with the sloshing teacup. The party disbanded with astonishing speed, and Robin limped shoeless toward the ramada. The cake was forgotten. Presents were beside the point. Ashen-faced little girls roamed the grass with their fists pressed against their teeth in empathetic solidarity. Parents began to appear out of nowhere to collect their children, as if summoned by some signal that bloodshed alone could activate, unheard by ordinary citizens. Julie, Mickey, and Rachel went along with Hope and a strident woman who seemed to be her mother to what Robin gathered was an emergency dental office, Julie calling out that Ron would come shortly to help Robin.

Then it was just Robin in the park, with the rosy debris of the party scattered every which way, piñata abandoned, the blood-smeared baseball bat forgotten where it lay. She made her way back to the piñata and retrieved her heels from the grass. Her hose were wet at the knees and against the soles of her feet, and green-tinged everywhere they were damp. She stepped into her heels anyway, then put on her sunhat. She straightened her dress, smoothing it flat with her palms. She gathered the piñata up in her arms and bore it back to the ramada, trailing cheap candy in her wake. There was a great lot of trash, and she hadn't thought to bring trash bags for the cleanup.

She closed her eyes and inhaled, held the breath, and exhaled, setting the piñata by the cake on one of the pink-covered tables. She put the accident out of her mind, with the ease of long practice. The sun was still high and warm, the sky blue, the park now peaceful, as she limped around the ramada, dismantling the party. She wouldn't think of the children. She wouldn't think of teeth. She would think of something else, a reverie, the thoughts she thought when she fell asleep at night, her French bulldog Moxie pressed against the small of her back.

It was a reverie with the anesthetizing familiarity of memory: in it, she stood on the Ponte Vecchio, looking out over the Arno. It was dusk, and the lights of Florence began to blink on, reflecting golden in the river, and the river smelled faintly of sewage, but there were also shops on the river, shops with espresso and perfume and pastries, and she smelled those things too.

She was younger in the reverie, and wearing a ball gown, which snapped around her legs like a flag in the wind when she scrambled up onto the stone parapet, for she was there not to admire the view, but to leap into the river, and she kicked off her shoes first, and, because they were light – satin ballet slippers – they caught the wind and floated in the air like bright small birds before disappearing from view below. She listened but never heard the splash, and then she held her bare arms out wide, pausing to glance over her shoulder, where she could see the dozens of padlocks lovers had affixed to the railing below the bust of Cellini, and none of them was hers.

Then she leapt, tumbling headlong like one of the padlocks' keys, shimmering in the twilight and weightless, hair loose and streaming. She landed on her back, soundless and delicate like a water bug, the blush-colored dress floating around her hips: buoyant instead of sodden, it cushioned her as she floated down the river, out to the Tyrrhenian Sea, the laws of physics be damned.

Laurel Jones

CREMATORIUM AT TEREZIN

This poem's been hiding behind the walls, under beds,
creeping along the sidewalk, staying in shadow.
It is dirty. It reminds me of day-old fish
in the dumpster—opalescent eyes rolled back,
no longer any reason for the catch, only rot is left.
It is grumbling—its belly is empty. I am still,
quiet. It passes by. I wait. It eats an apple and I
know this is a feral animal—there is blood in its teeth.
I imagine the flesh it took, how it must
have felt in the mouth, against the molars.
It dances in a circle of light and I try to tell it:
It is becoming cold here, the wind has taken off her shoes,
there are pearls of dew on your hair, flowers should
not be picked, and you are so, so beautiful. But this is a lie.
I tell it: I love you like I love the birds that sing in this place.

Anna Maxymiw

BARROW

I have the pickaxe and you have the barrow. We wear matching uniforms, both of us
digging a shoreline together on our one afternoon off, hollowing the ground for

gabions.

You usually harangue me until I shake, dumb and mammalian, in the lodge laundry
room, but now the work is hard, the sun chalky, and we are silent like bronzed water.

You're brown and green. Lucent. Hooks and bait, Rapala knife, contrary. Your mouth
sprawls. I rest the pickaxe on my boot-top, ask what you are. You say maybe quarter
-Indian. Should I get my status card? You just want to see me stutter, knock my

shinbone

with the blunt axe-end as I search for a handle inside of you to curl my hands around.

just stay under my hand still for one moment and I'll touch the cusp of your neck

where

your skin is smokiest—let down the sheet that is your door—let me pull your dirty,
smooth body between my hips on the bad mattresses of the staff cabin—let that

hollowed

silence sprawl out inside of us

BOOK REVIEWS

Detailing Trauma: A Poetic Anatomy
by Arianne Zwartjes
Paperback: 102 pages
University of Iowa Press: Sightline Series, 2012
Price: $18
Review by Aisha Sabatini Sloan

On the day before the 2012 presidential election, I tuned in to Iowa Public Radio. Two commentators were discussing the impact of the economy on the polls. At that point, I didn't think I could handle another word about the candidates, and I wasn't alone. A video had gone viral on the internet of a little girl racked with sobs as she mumbled miserably about "Bronco Bama" and Mitt Romney. Everyone in the country seemed to want to cry along with her. But as a new radio program began, a woman's voice cut through the haze with a tone as clean and sharp as a scalpel: "It always amazes me to hear radio commentators talking about the need for our economy to start growing again, as though it can be always increasing. As though increasing can be a permanent state of being. And as though we somehow, as a nation, are entitled to that. To that upness."

Arianne Zwartjes wrote these lines long ago, and in a context quite separate from the presidential race. But her words felt destined to have been spoken at this exact moment. Art was being given the space in a public forum to talk back. And its simplicity felt like a tonic. Here we are, arguing about money, poisoning ourselves with the back and forth of it. And suddenly, a poet appears. In another part of the book from which she was reading, Zwartjes writes, "every moment we walk around unaware and indifferent to the fact that a tide is pulling in our limbs." *Detailing Trauma: A Poetic Anatomy* brings us back to the body, to the wonder and terror of this thing that carries us around in the world.

Six chapters in all, the book engages like a medical textbook with human anatomy. The heart, liver, nerves and lungs are covered in a section entitled "Anatomy of Trust or Breaking." Adrenal glands, veins and burns are discussed in a section entitled "If Language Fails Us, or Body." And so on. The reader learns about the function and potential failure of each facet of the body, while accompanying the author as she engages with the philosophical and emotional nuances of what's relayed. We watch as though her words trace along the contours of a diagram, listening as she relates each curve and beat of the body to stories heard on the news, to language, to history and to the scenes from her everyday life. Zwartjes wonders, for example, if the heart or the liver best represents the quality of falling in love, using cultural metaphors as a frame of reference. Considering phantom limbs, she begins to contemplate the concept of loss altogether: "What do we do with the nagging pain of absence? Where do we put it, how do we sit with it when it threatens to trample us underfoot. A sobbing restlessness under the skin."

The throughline is a meditation on faith: how we live and love when we know all the ways we might be broken. She began writing the book when she was studying for her examination as an EMT, and also at a time when she was happily in love, both states bringing her into intimate contact with the literal and figurative notions of rupture, debridement and laceration. A poet, she teaches us how to love the language of the body, to confront the body's limitations, and to find hope despite the certainty of all that fracture.

I've read this book so many times, and the material never grows stale. As I read it today, the ice on the ground outside makes even walking a new kind of risk. I breathe in the news of another birth, another death, another bout with cancer. A book like this is not meant to be read only once. Like a spiritual text, these essays serve as a survival tool, a surface to grip, some solace in the thick of it.

At one point during Zwartjes' radio interview, a man called in to speak of his own experience as an EMT. He recalled an encounter at the side of the road. A person was hurt, and he spoke to them using sign language. It was the fact of their communication that seemed to stun him: a moment of union that would not have happened if there had not been this problem, this assault on the body. Something in this man's recounted scene seemed to speak to the nature of Zwartjes' book, which despite its clinical focus, conveys a certain warmth. We don't want trauma to happen, but when it does, we can see with sudden clarity the person sitting beside us. Zwartjes says it best when she notes that fracture has the potential to keep us "on edge and away from apathy. Slicingly alive."

Arianne Zwartjes is also the author of *The Surfacing of Excess,* winner of the 2009 Blue Lynx Prize, EWU Press, 2012, and *(Stitched) A Surface Opens,* New Michigan Press, 2008.

Venus in the Afternoon
 by Tehila Lieberman
 Paperback: 177 pages
 University of North Texas Press, 2012
 Price: $14.95
 Review by Lajla Cline

The narrator of "The Way I See It," the opening story in Tehila Lieberman's collection of short stories *Venus in the Afternoon* is a Catholic "Southie" named Sutherland, a window washer in South Boston who has lost his wife to disease, his daughter to comparative literature at Princeton, and faces the impending loss of his job—six months until a desk job or early retirement. Sutherland tells us that death is "like lightening—kinda unpredictable and cruel and leavin no explanation behind." Though Sutherland's thoughtful reflections about death are woven throughout the story, this isn't a story about loss; this is a story about what's left after loss, some humanity in us that keeps us wanting life, keeps us living, when all that we know and love is gone:

> It's funny how even when you think there's nothing
> more anchorin you to this life, there it is, like a rumbin
> in your belly and you wantin more. Even with the
> woman gone and my nights a long stretch of beer and
> TV, there I was, wantin more.

This fascination with what's left when we are stripped down is the driving force behind Lieberman's collection, a deft path of narrative that moves us easily through the many kinds of loss we face—of life, loved ones, marriage, intimacy, youth, dreams—past grief, to whatever is there beneath, something raw, but also shining and capacious in its unwavering desire to love.

The images of struggle in the collection are broad and varied, the subject matter familiar realities—cancer, isolation, adultery, oppression, trauma, the decay of relationships. And though each story considers the place one finds him or herself just on the other side of despair, an awakening to a distilled kind of love, the destination is not universally redeeming or uplifting, a complexity that rings true for any reader. In some stories the destination one stop past loss is hopeful, life-affirming—a friend's miscarriage brings a childless couple together in their desire for a baby, the death of a young man's girlfriend frees him from a paralysis he'd let take over his life—and in other stories the characters find that what's on the other side is merely an understanding, a knowing that somehow has value in its own right.

So, too, is the reading of *Venus in the Afternoon*, with its tender portraits of people we know, an act of redemption, a panacea to that ill we effort to keep at bay—loss, with its unpredictable visits, its unknowable scale. And in the act of reading we are reminded of Elizabeth Bishop's message to us of the place loss holds in our lives and its inescapable nature:

> —Even losing you (the joking voice, a gesture
> I love) I shan't have lied. It's evident
> the art of losing's not too hard to master
> though it may look like (*Write* it!) like disaster.

Lieberman's stories move beyond the practice of losing, beyond its unrelenting presence in our life, to show us that although loss may look like disaster, it can actually transform us, can, even, lighten us, as Sutherland explains at the end of "The Way I See it:" "And as the car starts speeding up, I feel so light, like any minute I'm gonna rise out of the car like a balloon sailin up to the sky."

Elegant Punk
by Darlin' Neal
Paperback: 116 pages
Press 53, 2012
Price: $14.95
"High Heels On A Muddy Road," a review by Pam Uschuk

I was a reluctant late-comer to flash fiction, fearing it lacked the character development I loved most about short stories, self-righteous that it was written by hacks who didn't belong in the real narrative/lyric poetry realm. I was wrong. Fine writers who cross that line between narrative and poem like Sean Thomas Dougherty and Darlin' Neal have proved me wrong. Neal's collection *Elegant Punk* grabbed me by the throat, swished compassion's soiled hemline in my face. Again and again, I was stunned by the depth and power of Neal's imagery, her juju at creating memorable characters rising from a swamp of poverty, abuse, and disillusionment to a clarified moment creating epiphany in me, the reader enthralled. There is no one I know of writing quite like her.

"At school she was Bitchy Boo Hoo. She was slut eyes. She was Fucking So Very Grave." so begins the story "Misty Blue Waters" that opens the collection. Misty is waiting for her rock star dad to pick her up in his limo and take her to a concert. Dad left home long ago, and Misty worships him and his fame. She's been "preparing for this weekend for two months. At least.". She dresses up in a poodle skirt and fishnet hose "because to be a little sexy was important for a girl", for their big night out, goes to a stripper bar her Dad frequents, talks to his stripper friends, drifts outside and waits. The story juxtaposes the teen's heartrending unrequited love with wonderful significant details. "She had painted her shoes silver with bottles of nail polish." Her dad doesn't show. In a power-punch of a final paragraph that mixes poignancy with a creepy edge of incest, Misty goes to her mother's bedroom, and in the mirror, she "teased an imaginary audience...wisped a scarf between her legs. She took her clothes off slowly, seeing the picture she made with each piece she removed, because this was art. She danced to no music. She wanted to keep listening for a limousine, just in case."

Darlin' Neal is both a masterful story teller and a poet who creates stunning imagery like "Crows speckled out everywhere...". Her language is inventive, her sentences rhythmic and elegant, "Over the deck, she flicked the broom at fallen leaves and watched a sweep of birds rise up as if they were in a groove together, she and those birds." In *Elegant*

Punk, Neal's full menu includes long stories like the unforgettable "The Upstairs Boy" interspersed by prose poetry and flash fiction. This is a collection to read and learn from. If you are hungry for stories that stick to your ribs and leave grease under your fingernails, read this collection and prepare for a feast.

Flying Carpets
by Hedy Habra
Paperback: 203 pages
March Street Press
Price: $15.00
Review by Alison McCabe

In "The Mantis," a short story from Hedy Habra's debut collection, *Flying Carpets* (March Street Press 2012), we witness one character's struggle to write fiction as it pulls at her reality. During a particularly trying time, she makes a promise to herself that "the next novel will not be about love." If such a book can exist, we might imagine it more rigid, watered down, but easier, certainly, on all of us.

Habra does not write it. Instead, she gives us a true gift, stories so fraught, so weighted with feeling, that they bind us together and compel us to stay. The boldness of her content matches her prose and, throughout these stories, she navigates both with remarkable strength. As we read, we see other sides of this world—from the Cité Universitaire in Paris to the streets of Heliopolis, and its nail salon where a local Egyptian woman shows off her powers of divination—and, while much of the landscape might strike us as unfamiliar, we still recognize these people and places, as clear as we recognize ourselves. Habra brings to life emotions we all know. Her characters are devastatingly human, as uncertain as they are obstinate. They search for meaning in a world that does offer it, if only by first accepting their inviolable capacity to love.

Habra cannot help but bring this humanity to light. Whether it is characters looking for guidance at the bottom of a tea cup, in the shuffling of Tarot cards, through the bearing of a talisman, or in their culture's ancient customs, answers are sought to mystifying questions. There are the fault lines running across generations, the misogynies instilled and challenged, the segregating rifts which are often, at the core, unified understandings. In "Distances," we follow the budding romance between a Muslim and Christian teen, and we see a mother set boundaries for her son when he, for the first time, brings a black friend into their home. In "The Green Book," a wife keeps written records of her family's spending habits, and finds this a tool to gain a quiet control over her husband. The wife writes in only red or black ink; she "refuse[s] to use a modern fountain pen. This way, the results [are] more elegant."

Flying Carpets dips into fantastical colors. As the collection unfolds, magical realism enters into many of Habra's stories with an effortless certainty. We begin with fairytales retold—in "Mariam," as a bedtime story, children learn of a young girl born out of a man's leg, and of a sister who, after taking her older sister's life, is haunted by her spirit in a mulberry tree. In "Anemone's Fingers," a child looks into an aquarium and "imagine[s] a complex world in which words [are] replaced by the vibrations of ethereal fins." This is a gradual shift, however, as Habra's fiction becomes not a room where fairytales are spun, but a book of fairytales themselves. A fisherman is trapped in a lighthouse by his lover's husband, and transforms into a condor to escape; a man leaves his wife and son, then changes into a wolf, just like his father before him; a woman swallows a bird, and speaks to let it free; a sculptor falls madly in love with the daughter of the moon.

In "Search," a character "realize[s] that words [seem] to resist the ferrets of specificity, escaping the initial thought, emotion or perception. Like oversized gloves, or those becoming useless over swelled fingers, words no longer fit the meaning, and the most difficult to harness, love, [can] never coexist harmoniously in combination with others. Its vivid and elusive nature remind[s] him of mercury."

What Habra captures in this collection is life's complexity. She is not only concerned with what can be seized, but what might also continue to evade us. There is an unwearying acceptance of our limitations and, with it, a sense of restoration, of having discovered some palpable, heart-wrenching truth.

Twitching Heart
by Matt Mendez
Paperback: 170 pages
Floricanto Press, 2012
Price: $17.95
Review by Kindall Gray

Matt Mendez's debut short story collection, *Twitching Heart* begins with the perfect epigraph by Octavio Paz: "In every man there is the possibility of his being—or, to be more exact, of his

becoming once again—another man." Just as Paz's epigraph promises the hope of rebirth so does Mendez's heartfelt, raw, and riveting short story collection, which focuses on an array of characters connected by the same neighborhood.

These carefully interwoven stories—which tie together seamlessly by the end of the book, but also function as individual narratives, with true character development and change—show how low human beings can sink: in one story a father is culpable in his gay son's death, and in another a veteran with PTSD brutally assaults a priest. Yet, the stories also showcase the great generosity of the human spirit: a son becomes a boxer to impress and please his father; a young soldier writes earnest, honest letters to his crush, even after she rejects him.

In the title story, troubled father Chuy attempts to reconnect to his son in an authentic way by teaching him to lay tiles. When Oscar is injured on the job, the reader is left with Chuy's sense of accomplishment, but also his deep regret: "Oscar turned to look at his father, and Chuy, knowing better than to turn away, waved goodbye."

In "All Anything's Worth," Perla, a woman descending into old age, steals a car after her house is robbed, revealing her desire to keep living, to have some fun and excitement rather than just curl up and die: "Perla hadn't driven in years but liked the way the car felt as she gained speed, how it was old but somehow entirely new."

In "Juan Looking Good," young Juan dresses up for his court date, and has a moment of true pride as he looks in the mirror. Later, he is left alone in his bedroom, and the sense that his loneliness might drive him back out into the streets, is palpable: "Juan listens as the train slowly pulls away, until the noise becomes a whisper he can barely hear."

Each story is bitter and sweet, wrenching and hopeful. The stories do not judge the characters, but offer insight into their experience and point of view. The men and women who energize *Twitching Heart* keep the reader coming back, as does the electric, confident prose, the innovation of form (including an epistolary, a flash, and a collage narrative) and the sophistication of the storytelling.

Another wonderful feature of the collection: readers get to piece together the "puzzle" of *Twitching Heart* as they read, because all of the characters are related, either by coincidence, blood, or just location. For instance, in "El Terible", Lena is a sexy tease through the eyes of a teenage boy; but later, in "A Girl More Still," we find out she sleeps around in order to feel loved, appreciated, special, and has a secret passion for poetry and writing. These revelations are especially delicious because readers can look at the same character from multiple perspectives, which adds nuance and depth to Mendez's already compelling debut.

Twitching Heart is a collection interested in revealing the human condition, with all its diamonds and blemishes. As David Foster Wallace once said, "Fiction is one of the few experiences where loneliness can be both confronted and relieved." Ultimately, these stories promise the possibility of love and rebirth even in tragedy, despair, and heartache.

BOOKS RECEIVED

Anticipate the Coming Reservoir, John Hoppenthaler, Carnegie Mellon University Press, Pittsburgh, Pennsylvania, 2008.

Blood Sisters of the Republic, Wendy Willis, Press 53, Winston-Salem, North Carolina, 2012.

Bluesman's Daughter, Jeffrey C. Alfier, Kindred Spirit Press, St. John, Kansas, 2011.

Choir of the Wells, Bruce Bond, Etruscan Press, Wilkes-Barre, Pennsylvania, 2013.

Contrary People, Carolyn Osborn, Wings Press, San Antonio, Texas, 2012.

Crazy Brave, Joy Harjo, WW Norton, New York, 2012.

Deadbeat, Jay Baron Nicorvo, Four Way Books, New York, New York, 2012.

Devil's Tango, Cecile Pineda, Wings Press, San Antonio, Texas, 2012.

Dreamless and Possible, Christopher Howell, University of Washington Press, Seattle, Washington, 2010.

Dreamseeker's Daughter, Carole Ann Borges, Alice James Books, Farmington, Maine, 2013.

Eating the Heart First, Clare L. Martin, Press 53, Winston-Salem, North Carolina, 2012.

Elegant Punk, Darlin' Neal, Press 53, Winston-Salem, NC, 2012.

Fragments, Blue Flute, New York, 2012.

Fully Into Ashes, Sofia M. Starnes, Wings Press, San Antonio, Texas, 2011.

Indios, Linda Hogan, Wings Press, San Antonio, Texas, 2012.

King of the Chicanos, Manuel Ramos, Wings Press, San Antonio, Texas, 2010.

Let Me Explain, Gaylord Brewer, Iris Press, Oak Ridge, Tennessee, 2006.

Light at Point Reyes, Joan I. Siegel, Shabda Press, Pasadena, California, 2012.

Lucky Fish, Aimee Nezhukumatathil, Tupelo Press, North Adams, Massachusetts, 2011.

No One Is Here Except All of Us, Ramona Ausubel, Riverhead Books, New York, New York, 2012.

Notebooks From the Emerald Triangle, Bill Bradd, Ten Mile River Press, Fort Bragg, California, 2010.

One Hundred Leaves, Blue Flute, New York, 2012.

Out Across the Nowhere, Amy Willoughby-Burle, Press 53, Winston-Salem, North Carolina, 2012.

Psyche's Weathers, Cynthia Atkins, Custom Words, Cincinnati, Ohio, 2007.

Rattlesnakes & The Moon, Darlin' Neal, Press 53, Winston-Salem, North Carolina, 2010.

Scorpio Rising, Richard Katrovas, Carnegie Mellon University Press, Pittsburgh, Pennsylvania, 2011.

Shimmer, Judy Kronenfeld, WordTech Editions, Cincinnati, Ohio, 2012.

Soul Talk, Song Language, Joy Harjo and Tanaya Winder, Wesleyan University Press, Middletown, Connecticut, 2011.

Strangers in Paradise: A Memoir of Provence, Paul Christensen, Wings Press, San Antonio, Texas, 2007.

Tennessee Landscape with Blighted Pine, Jesse Graves, Texas Review Press, Huntsville, Texas, 2011.

The Gathering Light at San Cataldo, Jeffrey C. Alfier, Kindred Spirit Press, St. John, Kansas, 2012.

The Home Atlas, David Feela, WordTech Editions, Cincinnati, Ohio, 2009.

The Light that Puts an End to Dreams, Susan Sherman, Wings Press, San Antonio, Texas, 2012.

Thread of the Real, Joseph Hutchison, Conundrum Press, 2012.

The Trouble Ball, Martin Espada, WW Norton, 2012.

Under the Lemon Tree, George Scarbrough, Iris Press, Oak Ridge, Tennessee, 2011.

Unsettled Accounts, Will Wells, Ohio University Press, Athens, Ohio, 2010.

Venus in the Afternoon, Tehila Lieberman, University of North Texas Press, Denton, Texas, 2012.

Vertigo: The Living Dead Man Poems, Marvin Bell, Copper Canyon Press, Port Townsend, Washington, 2011.

Vocabulary of Silence, Veronica Golos, Red Hen Press, Pasadena, California, 2011.

Walkabout, Diane Sherman, Lightbeam Publishing, 2011.

Waxwings, Daniel Nathan Terry, Lethe Press, Maple Shade, New Jersey, 2012.

When My Brother Was an Aztec, Natalie Diaz, Copper Canyon Press, Port Townsend, Washington, 2012.

CONTRIBUTORS NOTES

Alice Anderson is the author of *Human Nature, Poems*, awarded both the Elmer Holmes Bobst Prize for Emerging Writers from NYU and the Best First Book Prize from the Great Lakes Colleges Association. *Human Nature* earned a starred review from *Publishers Weekly*. Anderson holds an MFA from Sarah Lawrence College. Her work appears in the anthologies *On The Verge: Emerging Poets and Artists; American Poetry, The Next Generation,* and in the 20th anniversary edition of the classic, *The Courage to Heal*. A recipient of a Haven Foundation Grant for writers recovering from Traumatic Brain Injury, Anderson lives in Sacramento with her three children.

Charles Atkinson's first collection, *The Only Cure I Know* (San Diego Poets Press), received the American Book Series award for poetry; a chapbook, *The Best of Us on Fire,* won the Wayland Press competition. A third volume, *Because We Are Men,* was awarded the Sow's Ear Poetry Prize. His most recent collection is *Fossil Honey,* from Hummingbird Press. He has also received the Stanford Prize, the *Comstock Review* Prize, the Paumanok Poetry Award (SUNY Farmingdale), the Emily Dickinson Award (Universities West Press) and *The Ledge* Poetry Prize.

Devreaux Baker is a 2011 recipient of the PEN Oakland/Josephine Miles Poetry Award, a 2012 Hawaii Council on Humanities International Poetry Award and the Women's Global Leadership Poetry Award. She has received fellowships to the MacDowell Colony, Hawthornden Castle, and the Helene Wurlitzer Foundation. She has taught poetry in the schools and produced The Voyagers Radio Program of original student writing for public radio. She has led writing workshops in the United States, France and Mexico. Her books of poetry include *Light at the Edge, Beyond the Circumstance of Sight,* and *Red Willow People.*

David-Matthew Barnes is the award-winning author of the novels *Mesmerized, Accidents Never Happen, Swimming to Chicago, The Jetsetters, Ambrosia, Wonderland,* and *Stronger Than This.* He's written over forty stage plays that have been performed in three languages in eight countries. He wrote and directed the film *Frozen Stars.* His work appears in over one hundred publications including *The Best Stage Scenes, The Comstock Review,* and *The Southeast Review.* He teaches at Spalding University brief-residency MFA Program where he mentors in playwriting, screenwriting, and writing for children and young adults. He lives in Denver where he hosts the talk radio show *People You Should Know.*

Gaylord Brewer's latest book of poems, *Give Over, Graymalkin,* came out in 2011. Author of eight poetry collections, Brewer teaches at Middle Tennessee State University, where he edits the journal *Poems & Plays.* His poems have appeared in over a multitude of journals and anthologies, including *Best American Poetry.* His plays have been stages ftrom New York to Alaska. His next venture may well be stand-up comedy.

Jennifer DeJongh is a writer and archaeologist. She grew up in Ohio and holds an M.A. in Anthropology from the University of Cincinnati. She has lived in southern Arizona for more than a decade and is currently a staff archaeologist and instructor at Pima Community College.

Elizabeth Evans is the author of five books, including *Suicide's Girlfriend* and *Carter Clay* (HarperCollins). A new novel, *As Good as Dead,* is forthcoming from Bloomsbury. Evans's awards include the Iowa Author Award, a National Endowment for the Arts Fellowship, the James Michener Fellowship, a Lila Wallace Award, and residencies at MacDowell, Yaddo, and other foundations. Evans is on the faculty of the University of Arizona's Program in Creative Writing and Queen's University's Low-Residence MFA Program in Creative Writing.

Shaun T. Griffin is the co-founder of Community Chest, a rural social justice agency serving northwestern Nevada since 1991. *This Is What the Desert Surrenders, New and Selected Poems,* came out from Black Rock Press in 2012. He recently edited *From Sorrow's Well, The Poetry of Hayden Carruth,* forthcoming from the University of Michigan Press in 2013.

Linda Hogan was inducted into the Chickasaw Nation Hall of Fame in 2007 and is Writer In Residence for the Chickasaw Nation. Her many books include the novel, *Mean Spirit,* and several poetry collections, including *The Book of Medicines* and the book length-poem, *Indios.* Recipient of A Guggenheim Fellowship, a National Endowment for the Arts Fellowship and the Lifetime Achievement Award from the Native Writers Cirlce of the Americas, Hogan lives in Oklahoma.

John Hoppenthaler's books of poetry are *Lives of Water* (2003), *Anticipate the Coming Reservoir* (2008), and *Domestic Garden* (forthcoming, 2014), all with Carnegie Mellon University Press. With Kazim Ali, he has co-edited a volume of essays on the poetry of Jean Valentine, *This-World Company* (U of Michigan P, 2012). For the cultural journal *Connotation Press: An Online Artifact* he edits "A Poetry Congeries." He is an Associate Professor of Creative Writing and Literature at East Carolina University.

TR Hummer's *Skandalon* (from which these poems come) will be published by LSU Press in November 2014; a chapbook of unrelated poems, *Urn*, will appear from Diode Editions in the summer of 2013. His most recent published books are *Ephemeron: poems* (LSU Press 2011) and *Available Surfaces: essays* (University of Michigan Press (Poets on Poetry Series), 2012.

Richard Jackson is the author of ten books of poems and the forthcoming OUT OF PLACE (Ashland Poetry Press, 2014), as well as books of criticism, translations and editions. He has won Fulbright, Guggenheim, NEA, NEH and Witter-Bynner Fellowships, 5 Pushcart appearances, and has won the Order of Freedom medal for Humanitarian and Literary work in the Balkans. he teaches at Vermont College of Fine Arts and UT-Chattanooga.

Laurel Jones lives in Wilmington, where she works as a TA for UNCW. She is on the staff of *Ecotone*, and her poems have been published in *Poetry Miscellany* and *Body Literature*.

Don Judson is a fiction writer and poet who lives in Attleboro, MA. His first (and nobody will look at the second one) novel won a Bobst Emerging Writer Award from NYU Press. Judson has also been awarded a MacColl Johnson Fellowship, a 49th Parallel Poetry Award, and the 2012 Boudreaux Prize in Poetry from *Cream City Review*. Publications include *The Bellingham Review, 580 Split, Alligator Juniper, Witness,* and *New Letters*.

Cheryl Diane Kidder's work has twice been nominated for a Pushcart Prize and has appeared or is forthcoming in: *Brevity Magazine, Pembroke Magazine, Jersey Devil Press, The Northville Review, JMWW, Cobalt, Identity Theory, Map Literary, The Atticus Review, Eclectica, Word Riot, In Posse Review, The Reed, the Clackamas Literary Review* and elsewhere.

Andrea Lewis writes short stories and essays from her home on Vashon Island, Washington. Her work has appeared in *Cold Mountain Review, Harpur Palate, The MacGuffin, Bellevue Literary Review,* and elsewhere. She is the winner of the *Thin Air* 2011 Genre Blur Contest, and two of her stories have been nominated for the Pushcart Prize. She is a founding member of Richard Hugo House, a community center devoted to the literary arts in Seattle, Washington.

A native Kansan, **Kim Lozano** teaches creative writing in St. Louis, Missouri. She is on the board of directors of the St. Louis Poetry Center and *River Styx*, where she serves as a contributing editor. Her work has been published *in The Iowa Review, Poetry Daily, The Journal, UCity Review, Natural Bridge, and Discoveries: New Writing from The Iowa Review.*
Sebastian Matthews is the author of a memoir and two books of poems, most recently *Miracle Day* (Red Hen Press). He is currently working on a novel.

Anna Maxymiw lives in Toronto. Her work has appeared in such publications as *The Globe and Mail, Maisonneuve Magazine,* and *EVENT.*"

Toni Mirosevich's most recent book is *The Takeaway Bin* (Spuyten Duyvil). Her book *Pink_Harvest*, received the First Series in Creative Nonfiction Award. Multi-genre work has appeared in *Best of the Bellevue Literary Review, Best American Travel Writing, The Gastronomica Reader,* and elsewhere. She's a Professor of Creative Writing at San Francisco State University. tonimirosevich.com

"Philo Goes Home" is **Laura Knight Moretz's** first literary publication. Moretz earned an MA in writing from Hollins College. She has worked as a newspaper reporter, newspaper editor, and freelance writer. She will enter Warren Wilson College's MFA program in January 2013. She lives in Winston-Salem, NC, with her husband and two sons.

Mike Nelson was the winner of this year's Stephen Dunn Poetry Prize (*Solstice Magazine*) and of the Pablo Neruda Award (*Nimrod*) in 2009. His poems have also appeared in *Asylum Lake, Broad River Review, The Chariton Review, and Naugatuck River Review*. He received an MFA in Creative Writing from the University of Maryland and is currently finishing a PhD in English at Western Michigan University.

Maj Ragain has taught at Kent State University in each of the past six decades. His books of poetry include *A Hungry Ghost Surrenders His Tackle Box* (Pavement Saw Press, 2006); *Twist the Axe; A Horseplayer's Story* (Bottom Dog Press, 2001); *Burley Dark One Sucker Fired* (Bottom Dog Press, 1998); *Fresh Oil Loose Gravel* (Burning Press, 1996) and *The Olney Dreadnot Book* (Shelly's Press, 1979). He has hosted open poetry readings in Kent for thirty years, now monthly at Last Exit Books. Poetry is an ongoing conversation, yoking solitude and community.

Lawrence Judson Reynolds is from Concord, Virginia and has written stories and poems for over 50 years, some published, most not. He holds an MFA from UNC-Greensboro. This is his first published story in 25 years.

Joan Siegel is author of *Hyacinth for the Soul* (Deerbrook Editions, 2009) and *Light at Point Reyes* (Shabda Press 2012) as well as co-author of *Peach Girl: Poems for a Chinese Daughter* (Grayson 2002), Joan I. Siegel is recipient of the *New Letters* Poetry Award and Anna Davidson Rosenberg Prize. Her poems have appeared in *The Atlantic Monthly, The Gettysburg Review, Carolina Quarterly, Alaska Quarterly Review, Prairie Schooner* among others. Professor Emerita of SUNY/NY, she now volunteers at a local no-kill animal shelter, tends to 8 rescued cats, plants a summer garden and watches it grow.

Amelia Skinner Saint lives in Sioux City, Iowa with her husband, son and geriatric dog. This is her first published story.

Sharon Solwitz has published a novel *Bloody Mary* and a story collection *Blood and Milk*. Her stories' awards include the Pushcart, the Nelson Algren and the Katherine Ann Porter. Her most recent story appears in Best American Short Stories 2012. She teaches creative writing at Purdue University.

Brittney Scott received her MFA from Hollins University. Her poems have appeared or are forthcoming in such journals as *Prairie Schooner, Crab Orchard Review, Poet Lore, The Malahat Review, Water~Stone Review, Salamander, The Journal, Folio, Copper Nickel, Basalt, KNOCK, Jabberwock Review,* and *Quiddity.* She is a book reviewer for the *Los Angeles Review* and a poetry reader for *Blackbird.* She works in an independent grocery store.

Joel Smith edits fiction for *Spork Press* and every day is becoming a little more hirsute. It's not the worst; it's even sort of life affirming, like in a way that's to-laugh-at-death-seeming. His story "Anthropos" has appeared in *Wigleaf* and he's almost done with *The Parish,* a graphic novel.

Pamela Stewart (Jody) lives on a farm in western Massachusetts with 8 dogs and some others. Her most recent book of poems is *Ghost Farm*, Pleasure Boat Studio, 2010. Once she gets her taxes and spring cleaning done, she expects to arrange a small, fun gathering of letters between the late poet Lee McCarthy and Guy Davenport.

Daniel Nathan Terry is the author of two books of poetry: *Waxwings* (Lethe Press 2012); *Capturing the Dead* (NFSPS 2008), which won *The Stevens Prize*; and a chapbook, *Days of Dark Miracles* (Seven Kitchens Press 2011). His poems and short stories have appeared, or are forthcoming, in numerous publications, including *Cimarron Review, New South, Poet Lore,* and *Chautauqua.* He serves on the advisory board of One Pause Poetry and teaches at the University of North Carolina in Wilmington, where he lives with his husband, painter and printmaker, Benjamin Billingsley.

Julie Marie Wade is the author of *Wishbone: A Memoir in Fractures* (Colgate University Press, 2010), winner of the Lambda Literary Award in Lesbian Memoir, *Without: Poems* (Finishing Line Press, 2010), selected for the New Women's Voices Chapbook Series, *Small Fires; Essays* (Sarabande Books, 2011), selected for the Linda Bruckheimer Series in Kentucky Literature, *Postage Due: Poems & Prose Poems* (White Pine Press, 2013), winner of the Marie Alexander Poetry Series, and the forthcoming *Tremolo: An Essay* (Bloom Press, 2013), winner of the Bloom Nonfiction Chapbook Prize. Wade teaches creative writing at Florida International University in Miami.

Liz Warren-Pederson's work has appeared in So To Speak and Terrain.org. She blogs at girlofthewest.wordpress.com

$2,500 Awaits Winners of
2013 Lorian Hemingway Short Story Competition

• Writers of short fiction are encouraged to enter the 2013 Lorian Hemingway Short Story Competition. The competition has a thirty-one year history of literary excellence, and its organizers are dedicated to enthusiastically supporting the efforts and talent of emerging writers of short fiction whose voices have yet to be heard. Lorian Hemingway, granddaughter of Nobel laureate Ernest Hemingway, is the author of three critically acclaimed books: Walking into the River, Walk on Water, and A World Turned Over. Ms. Hemingway is the competition's final judge.

Prizes and Publication

• The first-place winner will receive $1,500 and publication of his or her winning story in *Cutthroat: A Journal of the Arts*. The second - and third-place winners will receive $500 each. Honorable mentions will also be awarded to entrants whose work demonstrates promise. *Cutthroat: A Journal of the Arts* was founded by Editor-In-Chief Pamela Uschuk, winner of the 2010 American Book Award for her book *Crazy Love: New Poems*, and by poet William Pitt Root, Guggenheim Fellow and NEA recipient. The journal contains some of the finest contemporary fiction and poetry in print, and the Lorian Hemingway Short Story Competition is both proud and grateful to be associated with such a reputable publication.

Eligibility requirements for our 2012 competition

What to submit:
• Stories must be original unpublished fiction, typed and double-spaced, and may not exceed 3,500 words in length. We have extended our word limit for the first time in thirty years to 3,500 words rather than 3,000. There are no theme or genre restrictions. Copyright remains property of the author.

Who may submit:
• The literary competition is open to all U.S. and international writers whose fiction has not appeared in a nationally distributed publication with a circulation of 5,000 or more. Writers who have been published

by an online magazine or who have self-published will be considered on an individual basis.

Submission requirements

• Submissions may be sent via regular mail or submitted online. Please visit our online submissions page for complete instructions regarding online submissions. Writers may submit multiple entries, but each must be accompanied by an entry fee and separate cover sheet. We do accept simultaneous submissions; however, the writer must notify us if a story is accepted for publication or wins an award prior to our July announcements. No entry confirmation will be given unless requested. No SASE is required. • The author's name should not appear on the story. Our entrants are judged anonymously. Each story must be accompanied by a separate cover sheet with the writer's name, complete mailing address, e-mail address, phone number, the title of the piece, and the word count. Manuscripts will not be returned. These requirements apply for online submissions as well.

Deadlines and Entry Fees

• The entry fee is $15 for each story postmarked by May 1, 2012. The late entry fee is $20 for each story postmarked by May 15, 2012. We encourage you to enter by May 1 if at all possible, but please know that your story will still be accepted if you meet the later deadline. Entries postmarked after May 15, 2012 will not be accepted. Entries submitted online after May 15, 2012 will not be accepted. Writers may submit for the 2013 competition beginning May 16, 2012.

How to pay your entry fee

• Entry fees submitted by mail with their accompanying stories may be paid — in U.S. funds — via a personal check, cashier's check, or money order. Please make checks payable to LHSSC or The Lorian Hemingway Short Story Competition. Entry fees for online submissions may be paid with PayPal.

Announcement of Winners and Honorable Mentions

• Winners of the 2013 competition will be announced at the end of July 2013 in Key West, Florida, and posted on our website soon afterward. Only the first-place entrant will be notified personally. All entrants will receive a letter from Lorian Hemingway and a list of winners, either via regular mail or e-mail, by October 1, 2013. All manuscripts and their accompanying entry fees should be sent to The Lorian Hemingway Short Story Competition, P.O. Box 993, Key West, FL 33041 or submitted online. For more information, please explore our website at: http://www.shortstorycompetition.com/ or e-mail: shortstorykw@gmail.com